FIVE BOOKS

Ana Blandiana was born in 1942 in Timişoara, Romania. She has published 16 books of poetry, two short story collections, ten books of essays and one novel. Her work has been translated into 25 languages published in 97 books of poetry and prose to date. In Britain a number of her earlier poems were published in *The Hour of Sand: Selected Poems 1969-1989* (Anvil Press Poetry, 1989), with a later selection in versions by Seamus Heaney in John Fairleigh's contemporary Romanian anthology *When the Tunnels Meet* (Bloodaxe Books, 1996). She was co-founder and President of the Civic Alliance from 1990, an independent non-political organisation that fought for freedom and democratic change. She also re-founded and became President of the Romanian PEN Club, and in 1993, under the aegis of the European Community, she created the Memorial for the Victims of Communism. In recognition of her contribution to European culture and her valiant fight for human rights, Blandiana was awarded the highest distinction of the French Republic, the *Légion d'Honneur* (2009). She has won numerous international literary awards, including the European Poet of Freedom Prize in 2016 by the city of Gdansk for *My Native Land A4*, published in Polish in 2016, the award shared with her Polish translator Joanna Kornaś-Warwas. She received the Griffin Trust's Lifetime Recognition Award at the Griffin Poetry Prize shortlist readings in 2018.

Paul Scott Derrick and Viorica Patea have translated all her poetry into English. Their first translation to appear from Bloodaxe was of *My Native Land A4* (2010) in 2014. This was followed by *The Sun of Hereafter / Ebb of the Senses* in 2017, combining her two previous collections, which was a Poetry Book Society Recommended Translation. Two further compilations will cover her other poetry collections: *Five Books* in 2021 to be followed by *The Shadow of Words*.

ANA BLANDIANA

FIVE BOOKS

TRANSLATED BY
PAUL SCOTT DERRICK & VIORICA PATEA

BLOODAXE BOOKS

ISBN: 978 1 78037 538 0

First published 2021 by
Bloodaxe Books Ltd,
Eastburn,
South Park,
Hexham,
Northumberland NE46 1BS.

www.bloodaxebooks.com
For further information about Bloodaxe titles
please visit our website or write to
the above address for a catalogue.

Supported by
**ARTS COUNCIL
ENGLAND**

The publication of this book was supported by a grant
from the Romanian Cultural Institute, Bucharest.

INSTITUTUL
CULTURAL
R O M Â N

Cover design: Neil Astley & Pamela Robertson-Pearce.

Printed in Great Britain by Bell & Bain Limited, Glasgow, Scotland, on
acid-free paper sourced from mills with FSC chain of custody certification.

CONTENTS

CLOCK WITHOUT HOURS (2016)

OCTOBER, NOVEMBER, DECEMBER (1972)

INTRODUCTION

Poems from Another World

Ana Blandiana, whom many Romanian critics have called the Joan of Arc of Romanian letters, is a writer comparable to Anna Akhmatova or Václav Havel for her staunch resolve to bear witness and 'to live in truth' while valiantly defying a totalitarian power. A prominent opponent of Ceauşescu's Communist régime, Blandiana suffered the persecution of two dictatorships. Her poetry was banned on three occasions and she holds the record of more prohibitions than any other Romanian writer.

Following the previous English translations of her poetry, *My Native Land A4* and *The Sun of the Hereafter • Ebb of the Senses*, this volume brings together her poems of protest, written before the watershed of 1989 – *Amfiteatru* (1984), *Predator Star* (1985) and *The Architecture of Waves* (1990) – together with those written after the fall of the Iron Curtain in *Clock without Hours* (2014), which presents a renewed poetics of disenchantment that acquires even more universal tones as it meditates on life at the end of the millennium in a materialistic consumer society. This collection also includes a less known aspect of her poetics, the mysticism of love, expressed in books such as *October, November December* (1972) and *Variations on a Given Theme* (2018). These two books frame her poetic career in a very different light. A prolific and expansive poet, Ana Blandiana constantly re-invents herself. She has distinguished herself not only by her subversive poems of political protest that speak from the heart of the Romanian people about their suffering and lack of freedom, but also by her reflections on the postmodern condition. Graced with an imagination that outgrows any specific political or national context, Blandiana is at the same time a meditative, visionary and intimate poet of love. Finally, despite her inimitable public sensibility, her most character-istic, moving and enduring voice resonates in her poems immersed in the mysticism of love.

Poems of Protest: The Metaphysical Aura of the Barricade

Blandiana's work has been conditioned by the grim realities of Communist Romania, so that, beginning in the 1980s, she often adopts a direct, bitter and denunciatory style, by means of which she has modernised the idiom of the social lyric. Among the poems of the 80s, the four published in *Amfiteatru* (1984), *Predator Star* (1985) and *The Architecture of Waves* (1990) – the last book to be written under Ceauşescu's dictatorship and the first to escape censorship – chronicle a traumatic time, a convulsed history, during which only the existence of poetry and defiance *ad absurdum* became substitutes for hope. Blandiana rejects the perverse mechanism of a discordant world, fractured by aberrations and anomalies whose protagonists are henchmen, witnesses and victims. In order to discover its illness, history is filmed 'in slow motion'. Blandiana's language becomes embittered, ironic, and full of direct references to Romanian totalitarianism. Intransigent, the poetic voice still bears witness to and speaks for victims, as Blandiana tries to awaken a nation from its lethargy, even though she remains aware that she cannot change the implacable course of history.

Blandiana's four poems published in *Amfiteatru* in 1984 – 'I Believe', 'The Children's Crusade', 'Everything' and 'Limitations' – mark a turning point and radicalisation of her lyrics. Her fiercely militant voice inaugurated the postmodern idiom in Romanian poetry. Circulated underground, Blandiana's poems were instantly recognised as the outcry of a collective despair. They constitute the first *samizdat* in Romanian literature. They elicited an extraordinary echo and became widely popular. Unknown people not only transcribed them by hand and spread them clandestinely, but some also re-wrote them in different variants of their own, adding new details of daily life from their experiences. The publication of these poems in an avant-garde journal, taking advantage of a moment of accidental carelessness of censorship during the interval between Christmas and New Year, triggered the second ban on Blandiana. The protest and international solidarity of Italian and German intellectuals softened the reprisals of the Communist regime against the poet and the journal, and in the UK, *The Independent*[1] published the *Amfiteatru* poems and explained their subversive bent to Western readers.

In 'Everything' Blandiana foregoes her oracular metaphorical voice and adopts a direct, concrete, objective and impersonal tone. Anti-lyrical and anti-musical, the poem is the epiphany of the banal and can be considered a document *avant la lettre* of postmodern aesthetics. Anticipating postmodern poets such as Mircea Cărtărescu, Florin Iaru, Alaxandru Mușina, Bogdan Ghiu and Ion Stratan, Blandiana inaugurates a new aesthetics of the quotidian, the colloquial idiom of the here and now, which would become the hallmark of the poets of the 90s.

'Everything' is also the chronicle of a stolen time. In a dictatorship time is not free. The chronic shortage of food, the cold, and power blackouts, among a plethora of hardships, create a collective psychosis, manifested in the slavery of unending lines. 'Time is free' says Macduff at Macbeth's death, but permanent terror creates a daily oppression that reduces the self to the condition of a mere object.

'The Children's Crusade' denounces the birth control policy by decree and shows how a totalitarian regime can control even the most intimate facets of existence and monopolise even the source of life. The poem alludes to Ceaușescu's natality control policy (Decree 770 of 1967) which forbade contraceptive methods and the interruption of pregnancy under penalty of prison unless women fulfilled their patriotic duty of giving birth to four children (in 1986 the number was increased to five) and allowed them to abort once they complied with this number.[2] Freedom is negated in the closed space of a totalitarian regime.

> A nation entire
> As yet unborn
> But condemned to birth,

---

1. Kevin Jackson, 'Underground Notes', *The Independent*, Saturday 18 February 1989.

2. Gail Kligman, *The Politics of Duplicity: Controlling Reproduction in Ceaușescu's Romania* (Berkeley: University of California Press, 1998).

Foetus next to foetus,
A nation entire
That doesn't hear, doesn't see, doesn't understand,
But keeps on moving
Through the tormented bodies of women,
Through the blood of mothers
No one has asked.

With 'I believe we are a vegetal people', an allusion to Emil Cioran's phrase, Blandiana opens a debate on Romanian national identity and on the form of resisting the 'terror of history', a theme she would develop later in *Predator Star* (1985) and *The Architecture of Waves* (1990). For the first time the luminous symbols of vegetation and dream acquire negative connotations and become the stigma of a nation oppressed by fate. Plants are a metaphor of a self who assumes the role of a victim in need of freedom – '(Haven't you ever seen / A yellow shoot / Entwined around iron bars?)' – and they 'are not exempt' from the limitations of the human predicament: 'illnesses… madness…hunger…fear' ('Limitations').

With the metaphor of the 'vegetal nation', Blandiana scrutinises a series of aphorisms of Romanian folklore and popular wisdom, exemplified by such proverbs as 'the sword does not cut the head that bends before it' and 'the water passes, the stones remain' (both of which advocate submission to the adversities of fate as a way of survival). With this phrase, she alludes to the debate on national identity carried out by such philosophers of the thirties as Mircea Eliade, Emil Cioran, Lucian Blaga and Constantin Noica. Indeed, in their discussions, the popular ballad 'Miorița', which best reflects the Romanian soul, becomes an unavoidable reference. In one sense the 'the vegetal nation' endures the tragedy of history because it cooperates with the ruling power and thus manages to survive at a biological level, but at the cost of spiritual existence.

A great number of Blandiana's poems have the ballad 'Miorița' as their subtext. It tells the story of a Moldavian shepherd who finds out from his magic ewe, Miorița, that two shepherds, a Transylvanian and a Wallachian, have plotted to kill him in order to seize his flocks of sheep. (The origins of the three shepherds correspond to the three provinces that compose Romania.) The shepherd, instead of defending himself or trying to prevent his fate, gives instructions to his ewe regarding his funeral, which he conceives in the form of cosmic nuptials in which the stars, the mountains and the seas will all participate. Miorița has been commonly interpreted either as a sign of Romanian fatalism and lack of pragmatism or as the illustration of the mystical solidarity between human beings and nature, a singular vision in which bad luck is not perceived as a personal historical event but as a sacramental mystery which allows the self to vanquish fate.[3]

In the *Amfiteatru* poems, as well as those of *Predator Star* and *The Architecture of Waves*, Blandiana poses the question of how to resist the terror of history. She launches a call to awaken the 'vegetal people'. In her view the self is condemned to consciousness. She agrees with Merleau-Ponty's idea that we are condemned to 'give meaning to life'.[4] In Blandiana's poetic vision, true transfiguration occurs in the awakening of a conscience that obliges the self to realise the spiritual dimension of its identity.

In *Predator Star*, images of pain proliferate: the light rots, and angels and people are overcome by exhaustion. When angels don't fall on the ground like ripe fruit in autumn ('Harvest of Angels'), they catch fire ('Soot'), in a universe in which neither rebellion nor sacrifice is possible. The 'predator star' in the volume's title is hostile to life. In

---

3. According to Mircea Eliade, though the shepherd cannot defend himself against his sad fate, he can give meaning to his bad luck by transforming it into a part of a cosmic liturgy. See Mircea Eliade, 'L'agnelle voyante', *De Zalmoxis a Gengis-Khan. Études Comparatives sur les religions et le folklore de la Dacie et de l'Europe Oriéntale* (Paris: Payot, 1970), 218-246, 245. Contrary to Eliade, Emil Cioran sees the vegetative paradigm as the emblem of a collective of losers who have never known how to affirm themselves in the arena of history, instead leading an existence below the rubble of fate. See Emil Cioran, *Schimbarea la față a României*,1936 (Bucharest: Humanitas, 1998), 9-10, 12, 39-41, 59-60.

4. 'If we are condemned to freedom we are to invest it with meaning', Ana Blandiana, 'O formă de protectție împotriva adevărului', *Apostrof*, 1 (236), 2010. http://www.revista-apostrof.ro/articole.php?id=1069

its first meaning, as a 'star with five fingers' ('My Hand'), it alludes to the red star of the Soviet Union, 'a star blown-in by the wind' brought 'like a seed', that is, as an ideology implanted by force after the Second World War 'to rule the night' ('My Hand'). But as a polyphonic symbol, the star contains, like all symbols, multiple antithetical meanings; and in its larger sense, it also refers to the devouring, transcendent power of poetry: 'insatiable', it has 'pierced [the poet's] brain / With harsh rays like roots', where it takes possession of her imagination but will reveal its significance only after her death ('Wind-blown Star'). By contrast, the poetic word leads an independent life and behaves like a mysterious being. The volume reverberates with repeated unpronounced howls. The speaker tries to shake the inhabitants into awareness – 'Everyone – the city, the country, the planet' ('Remember') – all of whom have sunken into a deep sleep. They lead a death in life and have almost forgotten that they 'are still alive' in their constant 'escape into sleep, into silence, / Into books, into drink, / It doesn't matter where, / Into hate, into love' ('Inward').

As an act of resistance against terror and a document of collective history set against oblivion, *The Architecture of Waves* represents, as Blandiana confesses in the preface, 'a reflection of a state of mind in which exasperation and humiliation, anger and hopelessness, shame and rebellion fused with a feeling that only an imminent end might lead to an improbable salvation'. Written in extreme circumstances, this is Blandiana's darkest book. In these lines the poet's personal destiny ceases to be a concern, while collective history becomes her obsession. When Blandiana read from these poems at poetry readings, an overawed audience would stand up as if taking a solemn oath. The poems have the value of a manifesto in which a tone of protest and sense of moral radicalism meld with the lyric voice to crystallise in contemplation. Blandiana creates the most complete dictionary of exasperation of postwar poetry. Although chronicling Romanian Communism in the 80s, the poems acquire a universal dimension: an x-ray of any dictatorship that reflects the condition of all who have been disgraced by the eternal 'offence'. Blandiana's meditations further draw on the philosophy of history. References to Dante, Nero

('Colosseum') or Ramses II ('Statues') denounce all dictatorships throughout time.

In one sense, *The Architecture of Waves* continues the themes of the poems of *Amfiteatru*, analysing national history and national identity in the light of historical symbols, myths and the folklore of Romanian literature, of which the oral ballad 'Miorița' and 'The Master Manole' are unavoidable references ('Fallen into the 'Sky', 'Without Name 1', 'On Embers', 'Binding Element'). Yet tortured by an alienating and degrading reality, the persona, an invulnerable conscience, goes further to examine without compromise the irreconcilable opposition between innocence and corruption, purity and debasement.

In *'Dies irae, dies illa'* the poet heralds the coming of 'That day / Postponed for ages' that will arrive 'Like a shining sword' in the prophetic tones of the Latin hymn of the 13th century, which will bring the liberation of all the oppressed on Judgement Day. Indeed, the great theme of this book is freedom and its predicate, the urge to rebellion. In a time when neutrality is no longer possible, even mere onlookers become guilty through inaction. In 'Melting in the Cold', they wait for the rust to open the lock that keeps them imprisoned. Here the persona becomes Prometheus chained to a rock, one whose sacrifice is in vain. People watch and wait to see how the waves will erode the rock and eventually rust Prometheus's chains, while his bones are reduced to 'Molecules of calcium'. In Blandiana's cosmogony the 'Murdered universe / Will grow again, / When the god that was shattered / Into equal stones / Will rise up as a barricade' ('Omphalos'). In truth, the only way out is through rebellion, and the 'barricade' is mandatory to enable the return to life of Omphalos, the god born of the world's navel.

Throughout *The Architecture of Waves* the central metaphor is that of the sea, whose waves allow nothing to endure. The poet associates the liquid architecture of the waves with 'this monastery always destroying / Itself like an echo' ('Architecture in Movement'). The monastery erected during the day but devastated at night becomes emblematic of Romanian history. The monastery, a key reference in the popular ballad, 'The Artist Manole', illustrates how sacrifice is an indispensable element of the artist's creation. The destructive waves precipitate the artist's tragic destiny, that of both the self and the nation, reiterated by the fate of the 'eternally liquid monastery / Destined to collapse at the shore' ('Ballad'), a shore which functions as a 'curse in the wall of letters / in which a nation is imprisoned' ('Without Name 1'). Furthermore, Blandiana rewrites the ballad from a feminine viewpoint. The persona enacts the drama of being entombed within the wall, as she assumes the role of the sacrificed wife on the altar of creation in the double role of victim and artist. The poem's speaker, Ana, embodies the quintessence of creative sacrifice, the poet's alter-ego, who takes on the fate of the artist Manole. She drowns the suffering of the martyred spirit in the voluptuousness of her own sacrifice and lives out her life as an indestructible symbol.

Although Blandiana's books are a chant to rebellion without hope, the poetic word illuminates the darkness. Even these sombre poems generate a magically powerful light, an aura composed of unmixed colours, a signature of Blandiana's oeuvre, which lends these poems a brilliant intensity, since their light is that of despair. Yet through their very lyricism, absolute despair gives way to faith in moral values and in human dignity. Against all evidence, these poems proclaim that ethical principles cannot and will not be crushed by tyrants. The world will regain its purity.

'Writing in White on White' in Ana Blandiana's Poems: A Howl from Another World

Clock without Hours (2016), Blandiana's 16th book of poems, represents an oasis of peace in a poetic oeuvre convulsed by revolt and disillusion yet always intent on maintaining a precarious balance between purity and the fall, between loneliness and a commitment to history. It was written after the successful *My Native Land A4* (2010), which has so far been translated into six languages (including English published by Bloodaxe, 2014) and which earned the 'European Poet of Freedom' award (Gdansk, 2016). *Clock without Hours* has already had an extraordinary reception in the Italian language. The book creates a necessary distance from the surrounding world in order to

21

construe silence; for as the poet contends, 'our time is full of so many words that the purpose of poetry has become to reestablish silence'. Within the scope of this silence, salvaged from the original sin of words, Blandiana's most recent volume is a book about Time with a capital T, time as the 'terror of history', and also about death, salvation, and escape from materiality. She reflects on the twilight of the spirit, the accelerated erosion of matter, and the evanescence of being.

Since 1989 Blandiana's poems have become more universal, austere and elegiac. Now her poetry modulates into a new tone of forgiveness and renunciation in these meditations on the fragility and vulnerability of being.

Blandiana casts her gaze on post-totalitarian Romanian society and once again affirms herself as the poet of freedom and solidarity. However, although her poems are anchored in the realities of her own country, they transcend the specific Romanian context to become fundamental existential questions and to address larger issues of our time such as consumerism and materialism. The poems of *Clock without Hours* decry impersonal human communications via Facebook 'likes', and the sense of alienation and depersonalisation of modern man, forced to live in those 'awful agglomerations/ Of beings unfamiliar with each other', or the increasing abandonment of rural areas in our industrialised era, the village being the spiritual matrix of Romanian identity. The present is felt as a series of lacerations, defacements and negative metamorphoses. Illness, along with its equivalents the wound, suffering and pain, are perceived as the onerous marks of individual identity. In a world of simulacra in which categories are continuously blurred, suffering becomes the only guarantee of authenticity: 'We live in a wound / [...] / The only certain thing is the pain/ That surrounds us' ('In a Wound'). Blandiana tries to give poetic form to the experience of rupture and undoing. For her, even maturity is understood as an excessive accumulation of life, an 'Overdose', which spells 'Exhaustion, like a mortal illness/ Born of too much life'.

As the book's title indicates, the duration of this universe is gauged by 'a clock without hours', an empty quadrant whose hours have been replaced by black holes. Blandiana's world suffers a continual decline, a world estranged, encapsulated within itself, devoid of meaning and values, where rapid material progress causes spiritual neglect. The poetic voice laments the constant diminution and deterioration of values symbolised by 'The obsolete sadness of leopards / Reduced to cats.' Blandiana writes with the sense of an end about 'A time without time – / A time named Never', which nobody can eschew, echoing Poe's 'Nevermore'.

The major symbol of the book is the cry, the howl, a postmodern version of Munch's or Ginsberg's expressionist cry. Existence takes the form of a 'Silent Film' shaken only by this howl that gushes forth from the depths of being to become a cry of life ('I Was Afraid'). The howl, the cry, pierces a world caught in the Leviathan webs of the 'genial spider', a web itself caught in a larger 'Web', just as time proves to be a set of Chinese boxes, in which the past opens up into a 'past that had no start', cannibalised by 'the abyss of another present time'. The howl encompasses the cry of the newborn child, a protest against birth, and that of the abandoned and lonely self facing painful solitude, vindicating 'The Right to Shadow'.

Moreover, poetic creation is another manifestation of the life force, its howl articulating a revolt against an unbearable reality of being dominated by a time that affects all levels of existence and exercises the power to dissolve everything in its path. Time is perceived as an illness, a 'mortal infection' that spreads from patient to patient, and leaves its traces on everything it touches.

The poetic imagery is composed of a modest décor of a declining world represented by peeling mirrors and distorted photographs. The void leaks out of hourglasses without sand while 'Curved Tiles', which once marked the 'The rooftop of the world', aspire 'To go back and be earth again'. At the other extreme there is nature – the sea, the sky, birds, wings, stars – to which the poet feels closer than to her fellow beings. In the midst of this abyss of forms, of concepts and people, the contours of beings prove evanescent and spontaneous. Thus, red leaves are birds, and angels 'the unfinished sketches/ Of plants / Whose roots you haven't had time to / Put into the ground' ('Sketches').

In the poems in this book we hear the voice of a self exploring her own selfhood. As if in a surrealistic tableau, the poetic persona discovers her multiple identities born in time and dreams, which she plays against each other in different roles, as part of 'a game without an end' unfolding across various level of reality:

> I only dream about myself.
> Though I'm several other characters
> Who terrify each other[.]

Dreams and mirrors are important emblems of self-exploration and a constant source of anguish. The woman does not recognise herself in the reflected image. Time leaves traces on the poet's face and soul and she prays not to be replaced with a spectre that does not resemble her. She feels that her most intimate self has been inopportunely socialised or raped by the other, dissolved in time. In anguish, she supplicates against this ontological betrayal:

> Do not replace me,
> Don't put somebody else
> In my place,
> Someone you consider to be me
> And you permit
> In vain
> To wear my words.
>
> ('From Mirrors')

Burdened by fear of the other, by alienation and loneliness, the lyric persona advances towards death, 'the river with one shore', which, however, is not the final stage of the periplum, but only another phase of the same existential 'Game'.

In Blandiana's cosmology 'evil', not goodness, 'is the seed of the world / Hidden inside a fruit' that lies at the foundation of creation and knowledge that leads to the inevitable perpetuation of original sin and challenges the self to survive among 'Infinite forests of trees / Of Good and Evil' ('Nostalgia for Paradise'). The rupture between man and God is not rooted in sin, but in the fact that man and the creator speak 'Different Languages'. Divided, the self is condemned to grope in darkness for its other half in allusion to the Platonic myth of the androgynous One, yearning to recover a lost primordial unity, now a poetic pseudonym of the absolute: 'Supreme and singular cipher: / Woman and man, / A self / United' ('One'). This aspiration for wholeness underlines both the loneliness of the creator and that of the self.

The only realm as yet uncontaminated by decline and degradation is to be found in nature. Salvation comes through nature and poetic creation, both cognates of the vital forces. Only nature can protect the self from the aggression of time and the world. The eruption of nature, the grass that sprouts 'among the computer keyboard' with 'its blades [of] ghostly shadows' in 'Green Icon' is a conception similar to Sylvia Plath's 'The blood jet is poetry, / There is no stopping it.'

Clock without Hours brings together postmodern postulations and a simplicity that goes beyond literary currents. Stylistically the volume marks a return to rhyme, and attempts a courageous re-creation of traditional verse forms. The poems experiment with various poetic forms: blank verse, classic rhymes, the sonnet, oral poetry ('Mândrămărie') or postmodernist verse ('At a Pavement Café'). With these compositional variations, Blandiana rehearses various poetic forms as if attempting to compose a poetry that escapes the dominion of time. She strives, as the metaphor of the title suggests, for a form of pure poetry that captures the ineffable: 'I dream of a poem the same as this event: /Or not the event, really, / But the wake of perfume / It leaves behind like a cluster of senses / That will never turn into word' ('At a Pavement Café').

Only artistic creation can defeat time. Furthermore, language must escape the fangs of time and stay alive, since, to use Pound's words, poetry 'is news that stays new'. Blandiana tries to renew poetic language by means of more intuitive, suggestive modes of expression that are more powerful than words themselves, and hence she resorts to an intensely metaphorical and paradoxical language. 'Between Seconds' is a declaration of faith in a new poetics determined to capture the ineffable dimension of existence contained between the covers of a book.

> Like a severed blossom
> Whose petals are wings, [...]

And how the seconds
Rushed like a brook
To help you get to
The heart of the book,

Where burnt-out stars
Are turned into poems

Blandiana strives for a poetic expression in which the referents do not draw on immediate reality but on the inner life of the soul; she therefore seeks 'just one colour that contains / All the rest'. Constrained to find a new form of expression, she writes 'in white on white', 'here and now'. Writing becomes a form of self-sacrifice in the name of goodness, knowing that 'Good is always / Hard to understand', and fundamentally opposed to the prevailing modes of writing demanded in times keen on flashy headlines in 'bright letters'. Blandiana's ethics makes her embrace the aesthetics of the absurd. She will write in vain, knowing that goodness does not make a good story. Aware of the futility of a text in 'white on white' that cannot be seen, that will remain invisible, that nobody can read, she nevertheless insists on writing her own soul. Her concealment is not intentional: it is the natural outcome of the fundamental impossibility of deciphering the depths from which poetry is born.

These poems offer a vision of the self's withdrawal from the spectacle of the world into a form of meditative ascesis. Wisdom does not reside in rational forms of knowing, and Blandiana proposes an alternative to Wordsworth's romantic critical assessment of rationality, 'we murder to dissect'. She opts for an intuitive mythico-magical approach, which allows occasional disclosures of truth and maintains its mystery intact while expanding its original unfathomability.

I go into the mystery,
But the mystery stays intact. [...]

Everything is shown to me at last,
Nothing depends on me.
        ('Always Led')

The poems in this book trace the quest for an existential condition beyond the mundane, in search of spiritual redemption. These expressionist meditations are above all a lucid rehearsal for the whiteness of the hereafter.

The Mysticism of Love

Despite her life and reputation as a poet absorbed in the life of the polis, Ana Blandiana's work nevertheless belongs to the meditative tradition of philosophy, and her lyricism remains steeped in mystery. Besides her prolific body of public poems, she has also written two volumes of love poems which rank among the most beautiful such poems in contemporary Romanian poetry – *October, November, December* (1972) and *Variations on a Given Theme* (2018) – the latter composed after the death of Blandiana's husband, Romulus Rusan, in 2016. Like Verlaine, who aspired to pure poetry, and Mallarmé, who sought the supreme idea, Blandiana in her love poetry continues to explore the mystery of articulating the language of the inexpressible.

Blandiana completed *October, November, December* when she was thirty years old, at a time that coincided with a period of relative freedom allowed by the Communist regime. She wrote the poems while visiting Sinaia in the Carpathian Mountains, in the impressive Bucegi range. The collection, an expression of spiritualised love, joins the great tradition of love lyrics in poems charged with references to the *Song of Songs*, Rilke's poems on Orpheus and Eurydice, Romanian literary myths of a fabulous youth who enraptures young women, and the 'Miorița' ballad in which the shepherd, in his precise instructions for his burial, imagines his funeral as a form of cosmic nuptials. Taken together, the poems comprise an *ars amandi*, but focused on the spiritualisation of love, though she does not extol the transcendent to the detriment of the human. These love poems can be considered a modern version of Petrarch's *Canzionere* written from the perspective of Laura, which complements the Italian poet's idealistic exaltation of the beloved, a mystical treatise that oscillates

27

between candour and lucidity.[5] *October, November, December* depicts love as both a state of mystical delirium and a reflection of the mysterious process of poetic creation itself.[6] The visionary imagination finds its correlate in a celebration of the lovers' nuptial rite that takes on nothing less than cosmic proportions.

The feminine persona is in love with an otherworldly, supernatural character who appears as a luminous figure in the indiscernible landscape of dreams. His identity remains ambiguous: he has no shadow, he walks on water but carries within himself a darkness with which he marks the forehead of his beloved. The oneiric lover's being becomes palpable only in the realm of words. He is 'born of the word' and exists only while she names and creates him in poetry: 'I cannot see you, I cannot hear you', yet 'While I talk to you, / You are' ('If We Were to Kill Each Other', 'While I Talk'). Love eschews the exclusive realm of the human senses to acquire a mystic dimension.

By sharp contrast, however, the lyric 'I' with 'the face of October' clearly belongs to this world. While he seems a lunar character, she 'come[s] from summer' ('If We Killed Each Other', 'About the Country We Come from'). The lovers have opposite natures and belong to different orders of being. While she is human, he is a fantastic personage obeying other laws, who arrives in order to deliver a secret message and carries the stigmata. But in order to come back to earth he has to give up his eternal condition and sink his wings in the dust, while she implores him to teach her to 'darkly burn' in order to identify with the shadowy side of his lunar nature. Their union does not belong to the world of generation and transformation, and is not inscribed in time. Rather, love achieves a magical dimension and gravitates towards a spirituality that transcends reality. As in the *Songs of Songs*, the lovers look for each other through nature, which defines the topography of their amorous

5. Constantin Ciopraga, 'Cinci Poeți', *Romania Literară*, year xvii, nr 32, 9 August 1984.

6. Dumitru Micu, *Limbaje moderne in poezia românească de azi* (Bucharest: Editura Minerva, 1986), 253-269; *Literatura română în secolul al XX-lea* (Bucharest: Editura Fundației Culturale Române, 2000), 187-189.

quest. They alternately find each other and separate with a longing that spiritualises the sensual in dreamlike scenes which evoke the visual transpositions of the paintings of Fra Angelico or Giotto.

The lovers meet in autumn, the season when nature prepares for its winter sleep and death, at the time of retreat into the intimacy of matter. The three months of October, November and December announced in the title predicate the denial of the sensual exultation characteristic of the exuberance of summer life. October arrests the explosion of vitality while still preserving summer's plenitude, just before it begins its agonic decline into losing its splendour. If October is the month celebrating light and vital riches, as well as being a prelude to decadence, November introduces cold, desolation, torpidity and slow rhythms, represented by the heavy flow of huge rivers. Finally, as autumn articulates the grammar of disintegration, December brings in a white month of snow, the final phase of matter returning into itself, with winter as a metaphor for death and catharsis. As an image of apocalyptic atonement, snow purifies time by begetting abundant avalanches that restore the world's primordial candour and purity.

On another level, *October, November, December* engages in a continuing dialogue with the famous poem, *Luceafărul* (1883), a poem with deep philosophical implications for the worldly as well as the transcendent nature of love, by the Romanian Romantic poet Mihai Eminescu (1850-1889). Eminescu's poem portrays the impossible love of Hyperion, the Evening Star, who falls tragically in love with Catalina, a beautiful young princess. Blandiana re-writes this poem from a feminine first-person perspective while changing the story line to intensify its mystic and erotic dimensions. In Eminescu's poem, a young maiden falls in love with the Evening Star and implores him to descend to light up her life and thoughts. Catalina begs him to give up his divine condition and become human like herself. In order to attain happiness through love, Hyperion decides he is willing to surrender his immortality, but the Demiurge does not permit him to renounce his immortal condition, an absurd price to pay for 'one hour of love'. Upon his return, Hyperion discovers Catalina enjoying the caresses of a young page skilled in love games.

Unlike Eminescu's Catalina, who yearns for the transcendent but cannot free herself from the telluric, the poetic voice of *October, November, December* does not ask her lover to sacrifice his celestial condition to become mortal like herself. Blandiana revises Eminescu's story of impossible love between the maiden and the evening star into one of mystical vision where both lovers relinquish their condition so as to be together. In Blandiana's version, in fact, they both change, he becoming more human and less transcendent and she less and less human and more ghost-like. Both accept this ecstatic transfiguration through death, which alone can abolish the distance that separates them. Death offers them the ecstatic transmutation of the I and the Other into universal rhythms. As in the ballad 'Miorița', death takes the form of cosmic nuptials that can annihilate the inexorability of time.

In many of Blandiana's love poems, her lovers become alter egos of Orpheus and Eurydice. 'My Shadow is Afraid' and 'You Never See the Butterflies' implicitly allude to Rilke's 'Orpheus. Eurydice. Hermes' (*Neue Gedichte*, 1904), a poem which renders Eurydice's subtle and inexpressible anxiety as she follows Orpheus out of Hades. In her poems, Blandiana nearly matches Rilke's notion of 'pure poetry'. She combines Orpheus and Euridyce's unease with the general atmosphere of suspicion surrounding them. As in the 'Miorița' ballad, however, the fateful sentence is passed against them and they are both doomed to be sacrificed. In death as in sleep, the persona loses herself in the Other. The ecstasy of love translates into a fall into sleep, into the utter possibility of beginnings, and into the infinity of an imaginary space that eschews the laws of time.

Since, as in *Luceafărul*, Blandiana's two lovers also belong to two different worlds, her love poems ultimately comprise an elegy. Still, the quest for transcendence represents a fundamental characteristic of her love poems. Since such love is virtually unattainable, it reaches an extreme intensity that projects it beyond reality. Eros is transfigured into a form of mysticism and divine illumination, and the mystical impulse sublimates the human condition. The lovers, evocations of Tristan and Isolde, consequently remain united forever in death, as we see in 'If We Killed One Another', where the lovers are described as 'killed and killer, / Saviour and saved': they find absolute union in the celebration of the *Liebestod* which vanquishes the death that brings them together in dreams.

In Blandiana's conception the sacred and the profane are not antagonistic but complementary, entangled in each other in a visionary panoply of forces. Death is seen as the reintegration of unified being in which all antagonistic forces meet their equilibrium. The motif of death as one's absolute fusion with the other is linked to the utmost expression of love, a paradox which alludes to the *Song of Songs* and the *Spiritual Canticle* of St John of the Cross. Eros in this scenario joins together the natural, the human and the divine.

Blandiana's most recent book, *Variations on a Given Theme* (2018), is a continuation of the love poems contained in *October, November, December*. It is an elegy addressed to her deceased husband, 'For R', in the form of an extended dramatic monologue written, as the poet confesses, in the faith of 'the inseparability that occurs through death'. The 'given theme' of *Variations* is the meditative exploration of love and death. It represents, as the poet avows, 'her most metaphysical book'.[7]

> Perhaps the word love
> Is too broad, too confusing,
> Too imprecise for what there is between us.
> It may have been right a long time ago […]
>
> But now, decades later,
> When there are no more distinctions
> Nor dividing lines,
> No matter how fine,
> And the word soul has no plural,
> To say I love you creates a division,
> Underlines a difference
> That no longer exists in thought,
> A step back
> From the only creature able
> To embody us both,
> As though we were determined to know
> Which of us has died.

---

7. Ana Blandiana, *Variațiuni pe o temă dată* (Bucharest: Humanitas, 2018).

With allusions to Dante, who conceived love as 'The force that moves the stars and the sun'[8] and to the Biblical story of Lot's wife, 'Only a statue of salt looking back / Among us mortal, dying ones', Blandiana fashions a new version of the Eurydice-Orpheus myth with inverted gender roles in which a bereft Eurydice laments Orpheus's death.

If you feel forced, as I fear,
To cross over Lethe,
The river of oblivion,
You'll look back at me
Without seeing me
And you'll hear me
Without understanding what I say
Nor what the syllables braided
Together at random mean,
It will be as though
You weren't dead
But I had died for you.

Lovers form an indestructible unity not only in life but also beyond it. The poem is predicated also on the Platonic myth of the broken original unity, according to which every human being is destined to recover this lost initial wholeness through a quest for the other.

The book begins with the image of the empty suit of a deceased lover. The lyric 'I' memorialises the life they shared together and transforms the absence of her dead lover into a real presence: 'What's important is to feel you close to me, after I forget that I've invented you' in a sustained effort to maintain the indestructible bonds of love against death.

Variations extends the beloved's quest for the departed lover into the far reaches of eternity: 'we'll search out each other for eternity in the chaos, just as we did on earth, till we're lucky enough to come together again.' In the poem we hear two voices, that of the poet to her lover as well as his voice mediated by that of the beloved. The two voices are entwined and fuse into one. The beloved encounters her lover in evanescent images of sleep, snow, dream, dying leaves and light.

---

8. 'L'amorche move il sole e l'altre stelle' ('the love that moves the sun and the other stars'), Dante's *Divine Comedy*, *Paradise*, Canto XXXIII, l.145.

Every gesture of mine
Traces a tenuous strip
Of light, that I can feel
Without seeing.
It's like a continuous embrace
From someone like me,
But it envelops my shape
And keeps me warm.
What an ingenious way you've found
To avoid abandoning me…

Throughout the poetic meditation, the lyrical 'I' substitutes the real absence of her lover with a desired presence. The miracle of being together is achieved through love: 'A milky light / Where outlines are blurred/ … / even when we cannot see each other, / We belong to the same time, / The same nimbus, / That we form a part of the same whole'. Lovers form an indestructible and indivisible unity that transcends death: 'there are no more distinctions / Nor dividing lines' and it is impossible to tell 'Which of us has died'; 'Only you were I. / Only you renounced the plural, / The multiple of two, / Only you knew how to construct a loneliness / Big enough for both of us.' He embodies only the other dimension of the beloved, the ground that substantiates the couple's inseparability in time.

Nature becomes a strange territory in which falling leaves are coded messages of cosmic realities which include life after death: The falling leaves light up 'the universe / With their all-consuming aura / Of parallel worlds.' The poem unfolds on a liminal space 'On the razor-thin edge of / The knife between parallel / Worlds, that writes and kills / While thrust into love to the hilt'. The lovers overcome the last frontiers between life and death, the here and the beyond, the past and the present, presence and absence. They meet 'in a bright, transparent / Bubble of soap' that the lyric 'I' 'sometimes manage[s] / To blow, / With the two of us inside' in the knowledge that 'everything only lasts for seconds / In spite of that, it's all so miraculous that / Who knows whether there, inside, / A second / Doesn't last / For thousands of years…'

The lyrical 'I' pictures the life of the beloved in the beyond in very factual terms. To be sure the very realism of her rational attempt to draw an accurate picture creates a magical and uncanny atmosphere. The beloved asks: 'Do you have seasons too?' 'Do you have holidays, too?'; 'I often wonder if what you knew here is useful there, where you are now, or whether you have to learn everything over again, like coming into the world and learning to walk and talk.' She imagines where he comes from by applying human categories and physical coordinates to the otherworldly: 'What I want to know is where you come from when I call you and where you go back to. Should I try to find the place in books, as the Egyptians or the Greeks imagined it?' She does nor cease to envisage their encounter in the hereafter as if it were a concrete meeting on earth: 'Now I also wonder… how we'll be able to find each other, where and how I could look for you in the beyond. The only possibility would be for you to wait for me at the border, but I can't tell you when and I'm not sure they'd let you stay there till then'. Stunning because of their simplicity, these other questions and conclusions – 'Is it easy to be dead? Is it harder to be alive?'… 'It's harder to be alive' – increase the eerie sense of authenticity of this interior dialogue and create a fresh poetic idiom with which to approach the topography of the eternal.

We learn that 'Everything begins with death. / But we just don't know what it is.' Death becomes a window towards a new form of being which presents in synthesis a deeply religious conception which conceives life as a never-ending continuum: 'And we prefer to confuse / The mystery with nothingness. / … In the space of a lightning flash, / And you see how long the road is / That begins exactly there. / So long that / You can't see where it leads'.

Blandiana advances various definitions of love 'What is love, if not the impossibility of separating two beings who have decided to be together?', 'And what is love if not a universal law that abolishes borders?'. Other tantalising aphorisms resonate in the book: 'The sleep of life / Consists of small fragments of death, / The sleep of death / Is a kind of resurrection at times, / And the sleep before being / Is the very substance that separates / The ages'.

As in *October, November December*, the lover is a Christ-like trans-cendent figure, 'a dismembered saint'. Worldly love acquires a mystical bent and turns into a yearning for the divine: 'With my eyes looking into yours, / Pantocrator'. The lyrical 'I' vanquishes the void created by her lover's death with her own means: poetry. She transposes her loss into verse because words connect her to the Word and to the Redeemer through whom the death of the departed lover is defeated in virtue of the divine promise.

Variations is an elegy at times, a letter in which personal loss becomes a victory of love over death, 'light against light', a reminder that the ultimate meaning of life is love. A poem about the continuation of love despite death into eternity, where nothing can break the unity of the lovers; their love resists all separations and endures forever. The couple form an indestructible entity not only in life but also beyond it. If the departed can be conjured up in the present, death can be defeated, and in this case the Shakespearean dilemma 'to be or not to be' becomes irrelevant, since death viewed as a 'passage between eternities' does away with all the limitations:

> Do you understand what it means?
> Now do you understand?
> Since you continue
> TO BE
> What is this passage between eternities?
> What is the difference
> When it's clear at least
> That it's not a simple question
> Of to be or not to be?

Variations on a Given Theme reads like a love letter composed of poems, journalistic annotations, and memories that compose a palimpsest of the poet's inner life where different time periods co-exist. The poems are transcriptions of a mystical experience of love which traces at the same time an initiatory voyage from physical absence towards a metaphysical presence. Rhymed verse, blank verse, prose pieces, sonnets, rondels construe a long poem which is one continuous uninterrupted lament as well as *Liebestod*.

*   *   *

From her earliest poems through to her current, more complex work, Blandiana's lines repeatedly assume classic and simple forms; they possess 'the nakedness of antique statuary'[9] while they compulsively strive for order and harmony, the principle on which her inner and outer worlds are grounded. As Eugen Simion says, Blandiana's poetry presents us with a 'tragedy in white, a drawing on a transparent leaf, a lament in a cascade of light'[10] in which negative powers radiate with a strange luminosity that glimmers even in the most terrible darkness.

VIORICA PATEA

ACKNOWLEDGEMENTS

This translations included in this edition are of poems first published in Romanian in Bucharest in these collections by Ana Blandiana:

Octombrie, Noiembrie, Decembrie (Editura Cartea Românească, 1972);

Stea de pradă (Editura Cartea Românească, 1985);

Arhitectura valurilor (Editura Cartea Românească, 1990);

Orologiul fără ore (Editura Humanitas, Bucharest, 2016)

Variațiuni pe o temă dată (Editura Humanitas, Bucharest, 2016);

as well as four poems first published in Romanian in the journal *Amfiteatru* and in English in *The Independent* in the UK in 1984.

Acknowledgements are due to the editors of the following journals, in which some of the translations from this book have previously appeared: *Chicago Review, The Cincinnati Review, International Literary Quarterly, Notre Dame Review, The Riveter,* and *The World Poetry Almanac.*

---

9. Alex Ștefănescu, 'Un om care un datorează nimănui nimic', *Vatra*, 1-2, year XLV, number 526-527, 59-61.

10. Eugen Simion, 'Preface', *Ana Blandiana – Poezii* (Bucharest: Editura Minerva, 1989), xvii.

Four poems from
AMFITEATRU

(1984)

Children's Crusade

A nation entire
As yet unborn
But condemned to birth,
Foetus next to foetus,
A nation entire
That doesn't hear, doesn't see, doesn't understand,
But keeps on moving
Through the tormented bodies of women,
Through the blood of mothers
No one has asked

I Believe

I believe we are a vegetal people,
From whence, if not, this calm
With which we wait for the leaves to fall?
From whence, if not, the courage to
Glide on the toboggan of sleep
To the edge of death,
Certain that
We can still come back to be
Reborn again?
I believe we are a vegetal people –
Has anyone ever seen a tree
Rise up in rebellion?

Limitations

We, the plants,
Are not exempt
From illnesses,
Nor madness
(Haven't you ever seen
A maddened
Plant
Straining to get its buds
Into the ground),
From hunger,
Nor fear
(Haven't you ever seen
A yellow shoot
Entwined around iron bars?)
The only thing we're
Protected from
(Or maybe we're exempted)
Is to run away.

Everything

Leaves, words, tears,
matchboxes, cats,
sometimes trams, the queues to buy flour,
weevils, empty bottles, speeches,
distorted images on TV,
Colorado cockroaches, gasoline,
flags, familiar portraits,
the Champions' Cup,
lorries with butane bottles, apples rejected after export,
newspapers, white bread, mixed oils, carnations,
airport receptions, Cico soda, bread rolls,
Bucureşti salami, non-fat yoghurt,
gypsies smoking Kents, Crevedia eggs,
rumours, the Saturday night series,
ersatz coffee,
the people's struggle for peace, choirs,
productivity per hectare, Gerovital, aniversaries,
stewed fruit from Bulgaria, the workers' assembly,
good local wines, Adidas,
jokes, the agents on Victoria Avenue,
frozen fish, Ode to Romania,
everything

---

* This poem unfolds on three planes: reality, ideological propaganda and
desire. It establishes a contrast between elements of lack and abundance. The
long enumeration of noun phrases with no verb and no full stop decodes two
realities: the official and the real. Ceauşescu's unrealistic economic policy led to
the ruin of the country, based as it was on intensive yet uncompetitive industrial-
isation, his systematisation plan (a Leninist goal of abolishing the difference
between village and city that envisaged the destruction of 14,000 villages, the
substitution of individual houses by blocks of flats for better control of the popul-
ation), the construction of the Civic Centre (a building as large as the Pentagon
for the government and the Nomenklatura), and the decision to pay back the
national debt to Western banks in record time. In order to obtain foreign currency
it was more profitable to sell all internally produced goods abroad, plunging the

country into extreme penury and creating a chronic lack of food while enslaving the population with endless queues for first necessity products. Romanians could only buy 'apples rejected after export' (since they did not meet quality standards), frozen fish (of Chinese or Vietnamese origin, usually rotten), Bulgarian stewed fruit from another Communist state, or Cico soda (Romania's version of Coca-Cola, criticised as the drink of 'the putrid decadent bourgeoisie').

Blandiana establishes a contrast between what could not be found – 'white bread', 'gasoline', 'matchboxes'– and that which proliferates in a bleak décor: stores with 'empty bottles', 'distorted images on TV' (television was in black and white, reduced to two hours daily and mainly related to the activities of the leader). The irony is that the items that abound in this enumeration, with the exception of those related to propaganda – official 'discourses', 'airport receptions', and the 'carnations' offered to the leader before and after his many visits abroad – are those that encode penury and chronic shortages. The poet mentions ubiquitous 'queues to buy flour'; 'sometimes trams' and 'lorries with butane bottles' that people are waiting for in vain; as well as the very rare Crevedia eggs (a special farm that produced and sold only for party members).

The noun phrases in this enumeration belong to different semantic fields: power ('familiar portraits' of the leader, a version of 'Big Brother is watching you'; 'airport receptions', 'speeches'); propaganda (big slogans like 'the people's struggle for peace'; 'productivity per hectare', the government announcing record numbers despite the poverty that reduced Romania to a war economy of rations; 'choirs', 'anniversaries', and the 'Ode to Romania' festival commemorating the leader's birthday or relevant dates of the Communist party); the apparatus of repression (the 'agents of Victoria Avenue', an emblematic street in the centre of Bucharest evoking Romania's independence from the Ottoman empire in 1877 is ironically occupied by secret police officers dressed in civilian clothes); simulacra and substitutes ('mixed oil', 'ersatz coffee' was adulterated with chickpeas; 'Bucharest salami' – instead of the Sibiu salami intended for export – was made for internal consumption from offal, fat and bone meal from various animals); pests ('Colorado cockroaches' ruining potatoes crops; 'weevils' present especially in flour and pasta); corruption and black markets ('Adidas', and 'Kent' cigarettes were made in Romania for export and became a second parallel currency from buying food in a store to bribing, obtaining favours or simply having your rights respected); disinformation ('rumours', sometimes official manipulations or false individual hopes of change); entertainment ('the Saturday night series'; 'the Champions' Cup'; as well as 'jokes', the only space of freedom and means of survival by which people could express truth, yet at the same time an evasion tactic and a mode of compliance that eschewed real protest).

The 'cats' recall a specific incident. During Ceaușescu's 1984 visit to the site of the 18th-century Brâncovenu Hospital whose destruction he had ordered to build the Civic Centre, his dogs attacked a stray cat which scratched one of them. Afraid of catching a disease from the dog, the dictator ordered that the cat be captured, an undertaking which led to a comic epic quest. [Tr.]

PREDATOR STAR

(1985)

Soot

What do you think about when you see
An archangel covered with soot?
Pollution in the stratosphere, of course.
And anything else?
That habit angels have of
Sticking their noses into all and sundry.
And anything else?
Stoves that get clogged up in spring
And start to spit out smoke.
And anything else?
Oh, now I've got it –
An archangel covered with soot
Could also be one
That's set itself alight –
Forgetting that angels cannot catch fire.

White

Falling and falling, and covering all,
Like a failed attempt
To begin the world again,
If the beginning was ever like this,
So pure, germination suspended, put off.

Falling and falling, and covering all,
The desperate secretion
Of a cosmic body
That wants to forget itself,
To free itself
Of its own image
That it just can't stand any more.

Definition

To be a leaf
And be obliged
To behave
Like all the other leaves,
Even though you
Know you can
Be completely
Different.
From this fact
– Strangely –
You do not draw the conclusion
That you're different from other leaves,
But that they, the leaves,
Are different from themselves.
This is a definition.

Twins

Twins in the womb of terror,
Dwellers in the same cell,
Blind and deaf
In the thundering silence
Where only the revitalising heartbeat
Separates us from the invertebrates,
From fish and birds, from beasts,
So that we can be born
In Its image.
Without the right to appeal,
Condemned to birth,
Alone and helpless before
Our growth, wrapped
In its expanding body
Like a grave that leavens future life.
The two of us,
Twins in the womb of terror.

You Move

You move through the mist
And I know you do,
And therefore the clouds
Don't seem to be cold
Insatiable coffins
That grow and grow to swallow up
All humankind
In a powdery fog,
Shifting and bitter,
That thickens the air.
You move through the mist:
Lucid and tall, a spirit that
Metes out meanings,
That garners worlds from death –
They tremble in amazement
As you effortlessly guide them,
Your hands on their shoulders
To calm their fears:
You move through the mist
And your eye splits open
Logical pathways
Through the chaos of life:
You move, love,
And I know you do…

Icon*

The woman with a child in her arms
Both of them serious and old
Looking towards the edge of the picture:
The woman looks innocent and sad,
Her son, with a deeper understanding,
More tragic.
United against their will
By the word *birth*,
Radiating suffering
In every sense the dictionary offers,
Embracing, helpless and alone,
The only thing that saves them is the love
That has brought them together
Not asking their consent
And – who knows? –
Maybe they're happy, supporting each other
In the constant terror
That makes them look
Towards the edge of the picture.

---

* Inspired by Cimabue's fresco in Assisi depicting the Madonna and Christ
Child enthroned with angels and St Francis. [Tr.]

Through the Air

Enormous moments, floating in shreds through the air,
And moving shadows on barely tinted snow,
I watched them form, and row across the land
And vanish in the light that brought them there.

Guilty of impermanence, multiplied reflections
Of chimeras on complicit snow, arranged
As though such fragile beings had to have a reason
To exist. Or, bewildered, wanted to explain

To eternity the peaceful, intense thrill of
Living as ragged bodies of cloud. Tall and austere,
Exterior to history, innocent of meaning and sense.
Enormous moments, floating in shreds through the air.

He Who Lives

Is it really so hard to figure out?
Can't you tell
From the number of fallen leaves?
Or by the rustle of the clouds,
Like paper in a breeze?
Or by these stones
That want to follow me, whistling
Through the air?
Don't you suspect, from my eyes, that
Look so much like the Eye,
From my hands, that look so much
Like the highest Hand?
From my wounds, painted
Millions of times?
Or by the arousal
Of the female trees
That want to recant their crosses
When I go by, before their time?
Forgive me. I always forget
That everything is pre-established.
Still and all, one last thing:
    Don't you know who I am
    From everything I've told you?

Lullaby

Close your eyes. You sleep too.
Just let your eyelids
Drop like a guillotine's blade and
Lop off the head of the world outside.
Close your eyes; say no.
There's nothing to understand in this lie
That's now begun to grow.
As high as a tower
Destroy all bridges below
And bury your final arms beneath the keep:
Close your eyes. Yes, you too.
A whole population, in a wink, has gone to sleep.*

---

* The last line was censored and changed since it was an open criticism and incitement to protest. [Tr.]

At the Other End

Nothing is finished yet.
Or does it just seem that way to me?
Shouldn't this leaf somehow
Keep growing?
Or the butterfly,
Shouldn't the design on its wings
Be somehow completed?
And these lines on my palms,
Are they only the sketch of
A painting that's just begun?
Nothing is finished yet.
Everything is waiting expectantly for a
Completion
Impossible to make out
In the blinding light
At the other end.

Insomnia Sun

White molten metal,
Hateful to the eyes,
Piercing eyelids,
Dazzling sleeplessness here
Among hopeless shadows
Keeps me hanging
On high, suspended above all senses,
Above the sweet darkness,
Promiscuous inferno
In the relentless and indecent
Light
From which I only desire
To fall, to fall...

Belatedness

It's too late now:
The cell itself is breaking down,
I know no laws any more –
The sunset is acrid
And the sunrise counterfeit.
A predator star is lurking
In the brightest moment
Of the acid sky, like a whimper
That melts into curses;

But its beam dissolves into dust
The wind blows quickly away,
Luminous grains of sand
That settle into every nook.
It's too late now:
The glow of heaven, if it exists, is only a theft
When clouds display
The entrails of heaven

Brazenly exorcising love.
Indifferent, the cell breaks down,
The light dries out of its own accord
Above a sterile universe
When the cry is death,
When silence is disgraceful
And the slender roots of the dark
Grip down into belatedness.

Inflation of Birds

The nest where foreign birds
Often lay their eggs
Has, at most, the right
To choose its birds,
But not its destiny.
In the annals of history
Since the creation
There is no record
Of a revolt
Against this universe edging
Closer and closer to failure
Due to the
Inflation of birds.

Inward

An escape, occasionally interrupted,
Between two anniversaries,
Just enough to catch one's breath
To be able to flee again,
An escape into sleep, into silence,
Into books, into drink,
It doesn't matter where,
Into hate, into love,
What matters is, it has to be
As absolute as possible;
An escape into the deepest part of yourself,
From the outside, from the calendar,
So that what can be seen,
At the most, is a moss-covered back
Or, when the wind is blowing
Two hands fluttering
That clap without conviction;
An escape that can't be stopped,
Always inward,
More and more inward, mustier,
And everything known for millennia,
The beautiful millennia of other times,
When we fled towards the trees…
Now we only flee into our own intestines.

March 25th, 1942*

That pain,
So very old,
That began at 5 am,
I hear
Those inhuman cries
And I atone for them
With life;
I pour my letters
Into this pain to fill
Its void,
But, more real than the history
Of the literature of the world, the woman
Writhes, screaming
Beneath the strictest command
Of the universe
Forced out
By contractions and wails
That her tears can no longer stifle;
That pain
Obedient,
I changed it
At noon...

* Ana Blandiana's date of birth. [Tr.]

If

If I had been created
To stroll among the leaves of mint
On narrow banks of streams
That flow through grasses
With ancient scents;

If I hadn't been made
With a bell in my skull
Whose constant chiming
Fractures the bone and
Makes up fears connected by rhyme;

If I weren't always given
The same maddening proof
That stars flow away and mountains soften
Beneath the great commandment
That echoes in my ears so often…

Courage

I look at my hands:
They're little branches where
Leaves, like eyelids,
Have never opened;
Wingtips where
Feathers have never
Dared to grow;
And not even claws
Have been able to come out
Like fragile shoots of a beast.
I look at my hands:
Like a handful of letters
That haven't got the courage
To pull themselves together
Into a word.

Nec Plus Ultra

I was told to search for you
And I, I only wanted the search.
I hadn't even thought about
What I'd do with you
If I ever found you:
Plant you in the earth like a seed?
Raise you like an animal on a farm
Counting up what I could get for your fur, your meat,
Your wool or your milk?
Or, on the contrary, would I let you eat me alive
Like an untamed beast?
Or would I lose my way in you
Afraid, as though you were a forest?
Or would I just drop down and down
And down in you like a bottomless abyss?
Or would I drown, and be eaten
By the fish, as in the sea?
I was told to search for you,
But not to find you.

Amber

So much light in the air,
So much honey in the sky,
The whole horizon looks like
A globe of amber
In which
Fossilised gods
And the unfinished projects of angels
Turn transparent
With astounding precision
And almost move.

The Weight of Snow

Trees bent under the weight of the snow.
Who would have believed it?
They looked so happy,
Dressed in elegant clouds
Made to measure,
That no one thought
To invent
Scales to weigh the clouds!

Union

Even now this union amazes me,
As leaves do in the spring:
All of nature is a miracle.
'It happened.'
What greater hymn
Than these two words?
Shepherds descended mountains
Through the snow
With flocks of astonished shades.

Chimes of Ice

You can hear it,
Can't you?
It's the music
Of the chimes of ice
Hanging from the eaves.
I can't make out
A sound,
But I know it's there,
I'm sure that
It's impossible
Not to hear it,
That this perfect
And evanescent
Instrument
Couldn't have been created
Only
For who knows what
Invisible, distant,
Indifferent
Listener.

Shelling

Everything gets smaller.
It all seems rigged:
Seconds fit into seconds
Like Russian dolls.
Each one dressed in the other's body
And empty inside,
To accommodate
Another.
Shelling faster and faster,
Hulls and shells scattered about,
Sifting non-existent chaff…

How Easy

If the gods were plants,
As Plato himself is inclined to admit,
How easy it would be
To grow them,
Take care of their minimum needs
(A few drops of water, a bit of manure)
Asking, in exchange, for
Flowers, leaves, roots, fruit,
Even the vegetal secret
Of the resurrection of the dead…

Sky or Earth

Sky descended to solid
Earth, matter,
Slightly flattering
Trying to look like dust
And it almost succeeds;
Sky in which,
If I could drill that high,
I'd encounter saints and gods
Buried according to their ranks,
Like skeletons
Chronologically arranged
In archaeological strata,
But no living bird
Is able to row its way
Through that thick paste
Where
I myself can barely
Move, doddering with
Half-forgotten gestures,
Not knowing whether the substance
In which I can hardly breathe
Is sky or earth.

Exchange

Like two large mirrors
Where you think you can see
And you only see yourself,
Meet your own reflection,
Side by side we
Flow, giving everything
And always receiving
What we gave, and until when?

On Principle

How sad it is to know
That you only exist inside of me.
I don't feel a thing;
Nevertheless, I'm certain
You're there!
Still and all, you've gone away
And I, obedient, care for
The lovely surfaces of
An empty statue
With ridiculous devotion –
Not the smallest crack
Where something could be seen –
And I wonder, at times, whispering in fear,
Are you there?
Even though I know you will not answer
On principle…

The Spell

I say to my eye, Turn into a leaf
Winking and blinking,
And my eye obeys, but forgets
To stop seeing
And out of the depths of the woods
I can hear it screaming vengefully
I see I see I see.
Well, if that's the case, turn into an
Eye again, I say in a daze
And it obeys,
But forgets to stop being green.

I say to my eye, Turn into a fish
Slippery and wet,
And my eye obeys, but forgets
To stop seeing
And out of the depths of the sea
I can hear it screaming vengefully
I see I see I see.
Well if that's the case, turn into an
Eye again, I say, feeling tired,
And it obeys, but forgets
To stop being wet.

I say to my eye, Turn into a star
Shiny and bright,
And my eye obeys, but forgets
To stop seeing
And out of the depths of the sky
I can hear it screaming vengefully
I see I see I see.
Well if that's the case, turn into

An eye again, I say, afraid,
And it obeys but forgets
To leave behind god.

The Scream

A comma, a few pebbles,
A smattering of snow,
A tenuous ray of light,
Some houses and leaves –
What modest props
To set off a scream!
The scream
Is straining to cling on with its nails
And always slips back down
Glass walls,
Trying to climb
Broken into pieces
Piled on one another,
Up to the teeth
Savagely clenched
In endless silence.

Towards the Mountains

If I went deaf,
Would the world suddenly seem as absurd
As a TV show
Without any sound?
A deaf God
On whom waters turn to wool and fall,
And clouds collide in silence
Like wads of paper tossed into
Heaven's wastepaper bin
Would signal the senselessness of
This universe that only exists
In the crackling it makes.
He would place
The giant palms of his hands,
That sometimes amplify
The shell of the ear,
On my shoulders
And slowly turn
My face towards the mountains.

My Hand

A leaf with five fingers,
A star with five fingers,
And my hand
That will not bear
Being beaten by the wind,
To rule in the night.

The Father

I don't decide.
Atoms turn into sand,
Sand into pebbles,
Pebbles are transformed into letters,
Letters germinate, sprout,
Bear words.
Words turn into animals,
They mate, have children.
I don't decide.
When I see a pregnant word
I never know who the father may be.

Questions

Why isn't everything mixed all together?
Why isn't the glossy skin of
The earth covered over with fur?
Why doesn't green and delicate grass
Grow on the burning backs of beasts in the woods?
Why don't trees have wings
And birds have roots?
Why don't the pebbles on the banks
Of the stream chirp happy songs?
And me, why haven't I learned to hate?
Why not?
Oh God, what a tiresome child,
Sighs the angel.

Remember

Everyone – the city, the country, the planet –
Was asleep.
After all,
What else could they do,
I was moved
As I watched them sleeping:
Some of them were elegant and graceful,
Others were rude, sprawling over the rest,
Others tossing and turning, wracked by nightmares
And remorse for not being awake,
Others, though, were happy
To have finally managed,
With sleeping pills, with yoga,
To fall into a slumber.
An ocean of inert bodies –
Stretching over streets, valleys, mountains
To the horizon –
Across whose waves anyone
(As long as they were awake
Or walking in their sleep at least)
Could make their way
(But to what?),
An ocean with no shores, motionless,
Almost dead.
Almost dead?
And suddenly a mad fear filled me
That they may not be able to wake up
At dawn,
That by then they may forget the gestures of waking,
That they even may forget they're asleep,
That ultimate test of being.
And I began to shout at them –
I begged, I implored,

Don't forget that you're asleep,
Remember
That you're still alive...

Body

Only a halo
Around a word –
A palpable halo to be sure,
And even voluptuous,
But no less insubstantial,
No less ephemeral;
A halo that can be whipped,
Starved, raped, killed,
Or that can simply die
By extinguishing itself
After doing its duty,
After shining like a signal,
Like a flame that marks a treasure.*

* In Romanian folklore, reddish flames are said to mark the place in the fields where a treasure is buried. [Tr.]

Wind-blown Star

From the very first you were brought on the wind
Like a seed.
I even joked: 'Who's ever seen
A star blown in by the wind?'
But later,
When you landed on my head
And began to sprout
I realised you were a seed.
Insatiable, you pierced my brain
With harsh rays like roots.
You are a seed.
What a pity
The plant which,
Light of light, you bring into the world
Will only be seen
After I have gone
Into the dark.

Soothing Song

Gentle dream of the hand caressing
A fur's electric silk
Or the pulsing of a tiny body
Quaking with trills
And even my eye that sinks
Through warming water
In its eye that floats
Among the leaves –
What a terrible mistake to believe
That the song that soothes
Was made by Orpheus
From words…

A Blinding Animal

Light is also flesh.
If you tug on it, it breaks
And bleeds.
Have you ever noticed how
A beam of light,
Dragged to one side of the sky,
Begins to rot away?
Have you ever caught
A whiff of blood
From the sluggish stream
That oozes out of a ray
Of sunlight, stumbling
From stone to stone?
If so, did you stop to think
About the heavenly pain
Perfected there,
At the heart of all worlds,
Where a blinding animal
Wounded forever
Keeps us all
Alive?

41

I count the green feathers
Growing from the fir tree's wings.
If it's less than 41
He'll have the right to fly.
But I get exactly 41.
This makes it more complicated,
But it only depends on me
To keep on granting this right.
'Fly,' I tell him.
'You're mad,' the tree responds.
'No, I fight for the rights of the fir. Fly!'
'Oh,' he says, 'you've clearly
Never tried to sink
Your roots in the clouds.'
'No. By the way, I counted wrong:
Your next feather is growing.'

1983*

---

* Ana Blandiana was 41 when she wrote this poem. [Tr.]

Compromise

The union of darkness and light
Isn't the shade,
Just as a marsh isn't
The union of land and sea.
Reach out your hand while you sleep
And do not breathe until you touch
My fingertips, stretching towards you –
Only our arms
Can form a bridge
Above the gap
While we sleep.

Continuation

The first thing I do when I get there
Is name the objects and creatures,
And they begin to exist
According to the number of letters
I've been kind enough to give them.
It's only a game, of course,
But who's not interested
In making something up
To forget that he's dead?

I made up the story with the letters
Given out depending on merit and rank:
27 is the supreme number,
The whole alphabet, the highest grade;
But for some I've left off
A dot above the i,
A cross on a t
Or a little foot on an m.

And so, of course, there's envy,
There are intrigues, a black market:
The little girls that braid the roots of flowers
Trade their letters for long rhythms and pebbles
While others offer ribbons of eternity,
The only material easily found
For two or three letters entwined.

Sometimes they rebel, they strip me of the right
To give out letters (but not
The right of the letters to say everything
In the ultimate charade)
And maybe they'd try to kill me
If they believed
It was possible to die again.

But only I believe
What existed before
Can continue
And I go on handing out
Signs, letters, words…

Axis

Raised up high between evil and good,
Hiding god at one end
And the anti-god at the other.
Could this be only a phallic revolt
Of the latter
Against the former?
Or maybe it's a bridge
In the middle of which, in uneasy balance,
We've been placed above the abyss,
Between the first and last moments of the world,
And it depends on only us to change something,
Drag ourselves an inch one way or the other
In the senseless balance of power?
Firmly planted on both extremes,
He is the axis
Around which the scattered and vacillating clouds
And the deepest strata of the earth
Go spinning
Like wings unable to tear away
In their flight.

Footprints

I follow some footprints. They're bigger
Than mine, and sparse,
Frozen in the snow
From a different, mild and tender time.
I'm going in that mysterious
One's direction, not knowing
Where he was headed;
I struggle to follow the trail
And the repeated clash
Between question and snow
Is like a voluptuous spasm.

My Eye

My eye is
An animal
That long ago
Stopped being omnivorous.
At first it was content
With little:
A few branches, a few leaves,
A flower, a breeze.
Later it went on to essences
And only berries, grains and seeds
Aroused, somehow,
Its interest and appetite for sense.
And now it simply refuses
To swallow,
It clenches its lids like teeth
Afraid of themselves
And will not eat a thing,
And it cries that it now has everything it needs.
It greedily devours
Large quantities of its victuals,
Proof that tears fall now and then
From its closed lids
Like a dribble of saliva, senile and innocent…

Outburst

With every outburst
A god is revealed
Smoothing the wrinkles
Of his long robes on the horizon.
There are so many kinds of gods
On earth
That we can't ever know
If we laugh or cry enough
To bring them out of their dens.
Laughter or tears,
It doesn't really matter:
As long there's an outburst.

Fir Tree Boughs

Spectral boughs of fir trees, waving in the wind,
Pennants of mist, prophets of a new and different end,
But who of us here will attempt to believe
In Cassandras born in the form of trees?

Standing still, while sweeping locks survey
Their homestead's travelling horizons,
The truth they couldn't first believe melts
Away into sap from grinding moans.

Even in their dreams they will not leave
While water and sky, around them, go.
'You come too,' the wind pleads constantly.
The boughs burst out: 'But this is our home.'

Harvest of Angels

…Every now and then
A dull thump
Like falling
Fruit on the grass.
How quickly time passes!
The angels are already ripe
And beginning to fall.
It must be autumn in heaven…

The Bell That I Hear

The bell that I hear –
It tolls so far away
I cannot tell if its voice
Rings out
Through earth, or sky, or sea,
Like an animal's voice
Tired of death,
It drags itself a few feet more
Towards its shelter-grave
Which can hide it and hold it,
This terrible hiding place
That I am
Where it dies
Every time
Before it can say
Where the bell is,
Whose it is and why
It began to toll…

Shore

Sleep beats like an ocean and rhythmically
Pounds the living shore that I am, and sight
Grows dim, and I nod, and I write
With the thorns of my eyelids cunningly down;

I dredge a syllable from waters, bland
Soft earth of sleep. An older one is near.
The ocean sets off chants in my ear and
Rhythmically beats the shore that I am.

I crumble with a letter, a word, a year, and then
Over calendars I droop and drowse again,
While sleep keeps pulsing like an ocean on
The shore, crumpling this disfigured poem.

Letters

This fear of flowing
From A,
Never flowing towards A,
This fear
Of going through
All the letters of the alphabet
That you already know from others,
Because others have gone through them
Trying their luck,
Each one in their own way,
Up to Q, up to T,
And the luckiest ones all the way up to Z,
Although no one ever flowed
Backwards,
No one ever managed to ripple back
Before A,
No one is even able to imagine
What there is before or after the alphabet:
More letters?
More letters?
More letters?

Dance

The letter betrays
The silence lies
The sign is vague
The cry is false
The whisper is unsafe
The eye is a cheat
The embrace
Is only a dance.

Messages diseased
Ciphers lost
High and low
Far and wide
The sky-blue sky
Is only the depth
Of the heavy cover
Of nothingness.

Scale with a Single Pan

I'm only guilty of what I haven't done.
Tropical forests have grown among the columns
Of temples I haven't prayed in,
Oceans of tears
In which I refused to be buried,
Enemies I refused to hate,
Swords I refused to wield,
Words I never learned to shout,
Bodies I haven't loved,
Beasts I didn't kill,
Mountains I never climbed,
Ornate museums in the buds of lilies
That I never smelled!
They all have the right to accuse me,
And my deeds, no matter how good,
Will never be enough to reach
A balance, even if unsteady,
Since the final scales
Will not measure evil and good,
But only what was and what wasn't.

Tale

I walk with care, and slow,
On a path
That I myself make
With every step:
To be able to get back
I leave a trail
Of crumbs of letters and words.
I started some time back
And ran out of
The syllables I had
As provisions for the road.
Luckily, I discovered
That everything
Can be turned into words
And I kept on walking
And crumbling
The words that unravel me
As a sweater unravels
Frayed wool from too much wear…

The Number of Birds

What did I forget?
My God, what did I forget?
Soul-birds fly from
Me when I sleep,
But the same ones don't come back
To this nest that I am,
Or, maybe
I'm never sure
If I'm the same.
Always this overwhelming feeling
That I've forgotten something,
That something has been lost
From the endless sequence of existences
That I counted
By the number of birds.

Wail

Close the eye, that empty eye
That's always open at the top
Of the altarpiece,
Sign of nothing but the gaze,
Now blind,
Frozen in its first belief.

Close the eye, do something,
Move your pupil, just a bit, beneath the smoke,
Lower, slowly, your eyelid,
Scratch the ancient colour
With your lashes
To show that you understand.

Surmise

Is the flower free
If the date it has to bloom
And the date it will wither,
The perfume
It must give off
And the colour it has to show
Have all been precisely set?
The flower says yes.
And the petals say yes, each one,
And the stamens, and the tiny threads of pollen
And the leaves, and the slender and fragile tower
Of the neck. Yes.
But then, what is freedom? I ask
Somewhat flustered, already surmising the answer.
What a question! Amazed
The angel blinks its petals in reply.

THE ARCHITECTURE OF WAVES

(1990)

This book was completed in 1987, and some of the poems in it were published in various journals thanks to the courage and solidarity of their editors during the spring and summer of the following year, until the ban in August 1988.

The book is a reflection of a state of mind in which exasperation and humiliation, anger and hopelessness, shame and rebellion fused with a feeling that only an imminent end might lead to an improbable salvation.

Freedom has transformed these pages, which were initially handwritten manifestos or documents concerning the collective memory that had to be read between the lines, into simple poems which only aspire to endure as aesthetic works.

I dedicate them to those who, at the cost of their lives, have also made possible the return of poetry for its own sake.

28 December 1989

A Trap

Here's what I'll do:
Instead of a stone, a mirror.
And instead of a name,
Another mirror that looks the same.
It'll be a kind of trap
You'll fall into
In the end.
I don't care if nobody knows
Where my grave is,
When you bend down
Curious to see
Who it could be
And you see
Yourselves.

Architecture in Motion

Who and what could ever stop
This architecture in motion
Always born again and dying,
This monastery coming towards
Me, that swells and grows, and is here,
With vaults and domes of foam
Suspended like a wreath of crowns
That leap into the air, and slowly disperse, and collapse,
And fall apart in a cloud of jellyfish and crabs
And drain into the earth?

Who could ever paralyse
This motion too alive to die
And too mortal not to come back to life again and again,
Who could shout to the waves, 'Be still!'
And order the waters not to be seas,
And this monastery always destroying
Itself like an echo
That broods over ossified columns
In the egg of the surrounding air.

Signal

Stop,
Move no more,
Stop right there!
Every motion
Is a degradation.
A fruit is the putrefication
Of the idea born in a blossom,
And conception, the first false step
Of those who love and are loved.

Stop,
Move no more,
Hold at bay
In your peasant chrysalis
The fateful butterfly that
Shuttles every day.
But who can halt
The ceaseless heaving fall
Of water on the shore…

Stop,
Change no more,
In the hope
That no one and nothing else will die:
Other, much worse killers
Would be born,
And the little dwarf
Would be smaller still.

When waves have shattered on rock,
It's braver to halt the hands of the clock.

Earthquake *

The earth shuddered, hysterical, upset,
An earth with waves
Like the sea,
The mystery struggling to keep
Its soul of fire
Hidden in the grain,
Predator both rich and vulnerable, able
To mix ancestral ruins
With terror and future rubble with fear...
And yet, what else but a wave
Could be born of another wave,
Destroyed and willing to begin
Again?
Native earth
Smashed to bits
Through which time at random passes
Turning into history
As it goes...

---

* Allusion to the earthquake that shook Bucharest on 4 March 1977 (7.2 magnitude on the Richter scale) killing 1,578 and wounding 11,300. Blandiana's husband, Romulus Rusan, lived in one of those buildings that collapsed, and miraculously survived a fall from the seventh floor to the fourth. [Tr.]

Passage

Everything changes,
Has changed
Or will change,
Rocks grow roots
And sprout,
And then, according to some beliefs,
Begin to slowly move,
Peasants graft daily vouchers for the train
On the handles of dried-out ploughs.
Aha!
Plants with claws and wings try hard
To save the seeds, now used to passing
From one set of laws to another,
The long flight of clouds through the earth,
Pulsing chlorophyll,
Fishes singing on the boughs,
And the idling engine of the breadmaker's truck
At the edge of the field;
Meanwhile,
Epoch of passage,
Eternity
As far from the past
As the future...

My Forehead

My forehead is a rock
Where the ebb and flow of
The waves comes and goes,
They wash it and erode it,
They sculpt it
And wear it down into sand,
Their waters run through
The shrinking grooves,
More and more featureless,
Back and forth
In the light of the waning moon –
A rock that disappeared
Forgotten long ago
Beneath the insulting motion, eternal
Ebb and flow.

The Hour

My silver bones
Around which
Suns, in widening gyres
Illuminate hopelessness,
I feel it coming closer,
That hour so often announced.
Everything is ready, Master,
Place the mute generations of your slaves
In formation
Beneath the mast.
The waves of the sea retract
Like wasted gums
From rotting teeth.

Dies ille, dies irae*

It will come,
It has to come,
That day
Postponed for ages
Will arrive,
It's going to come,
It's getting closer,
You can hear
Its beating pulse
On the horizon,
It will come,
It's in the air,
It can't be put off any longer,
Have no doubt, it will come,
That day
Like a shining sword
In the blinding light.

---

* 'Dies irae, dies illa,/ Solvet sæclum in favilla,/ Teste David cum Sibylla!'
('Day of wrath and doom impending, / David's word with Sibyl's blending,/
Heaven and earth in ashes ending'), 'Dies Irae' ('Day of Wrath'), anonymous
Latin hymn of the 13th century that announces the Last Judgement which will
bring justice. This poem was published on the first page of *România liberă*, the
most important Romanian newspaper, on the first day after the fall of the
Communist government in 1989. [Tr.]

Cold Casting

Decades of waiting
For the key to turn in the lock;
Rustier and rustier,
Looking on for decades
Without a word,
Without a destiny.
From time to time,
It seems to turn, just a bit,
And then –
Oh, the diversity of voices
After the illusion of movement:
Those who thought
It moved forward,
Those who thought
It moved back,
And some who thought not moving at all
Would be the best bet…
Who and what could stop
The chimera?
But no,
Only the rust went on
In the heart of the lock,
Cold casting,
Red dust replacing the bolt
Molecule by molecule
(And again the chorus of signs,
Conjectures, opinions:
In a century, in two,
In a millennium…)
History in slow motion.

The Path

Pillars bending with age, old bones
In faded flesh beneath the lime,
Cavities and sandy tunnels grown
Into the wood of an exhausted time

And the eaves of roofs made weak by the years
Where swifts no longer dare to alight –
Who, if they moan, will we scorn when we hear?
On whom take revenge for renouncing the fight?

Who will hold back from pursuing this way –
The only path we must not avoid,
When look! beneath the bulldozer's blade
The final poem is destroyed

Like a broken hourglass, unable now
To measure pain and misery?
A cry postponed and rotting out,
A beggar's cry to history…

Tableau

There are six or seven
With their snouts stuck
Into the same dead prey,
Their bodies made longer
By those terrifying slithering tails
Like the spokes of a wheel
On the asphalt,
Forming a sun
With fat, quivering rays,
Risen from the canal.
A sun of rats
In the asphalt sky,
Apollo of garbage, a future
Star with fur for
A different age of sewers and drains
Trickling towards the day of hereafter,
A rodent god
That gobbles up the years
With a halo
Of garbage…

Of Love

Don't go. Please stay. Sit here by my side
And hold my head so I won't be afraid
When the tedious sleep I'm condemned to
Sharpens and twists like a nightmare blade.

Cradle my temples in your hands like
A chalice; raise it gently to your mouth
And place your lips on mine:
Take in the scream that I let out,

So then we may not hear the sobs
That form the contours of my flesh.
Embrace me to smother this wave of fear
That rises all around me in a rush

And take it all away, and only leave
The empty quotes and broken shards,
And let them writhe in sickness and die
And the sun and the other stars…*

---

* Allusion to the last line of Dante's *Divine Comedy*, 'L'amor che move il sole
e l'altre stelle' ('the love that moves the sun and the other stars'), *Paradise*, Canto
XXXIII, l.145. [Tr.]

Omphalos

A stone is a god that
Moves so slowly
My swiftly dying eye
Cannot
Perceive the motion,
As we cannot ask
A wave,
A cloud
To understand the ocean.
When everything collapses
And afterwards dissolves
Into a poisonous mixture
Of yesterday and tomorrow,
A stone is a seed of the world
Still alive,
The shrivelled sense that remains,
Omphalos and bud, from which the whole
Murdered universe
Will grow again,
When the god that was shattered
Into equal stones
Will rise up as a barricade.

Worms on the Move*

Worms on the move, on wings, on wheels,
Assigned to
A newer, more
Modern cemetery;
Waves of worms
In ancient corpses moved
To a vaguer eternity
Of a secular hell;
Waves of worms
That migrate to new crypts,
Worms on the move, on their way
To the day of hereafter,
While in a firmer future lake,
The fish will learn to be worms.

---

* In the 80s, Ceauşescu's 'systematisation plan' caused the destruction of the old centre of Bucharest and the displacement of two cemeteries, Crângaşi and Băneasa. [Tr.]

Sleep

What sweet revenge!
The last of the slaves,
Who cannot even imagine
That he's free
And begins to tremble
At only the thought
Of making
The slightest gesture of revolt,
Escapes
By simply closing his eyes,
Evades all kinds of control,
And flees.
He can't be pursued
Because his master
Is always left behind
On the shore,
Furiously biting his fists
And watching,
With insomnia.

Subject

To discover you're
Enclosed in a comparison
Like a cage
You've built
Around yourself
And where you can't live any longer,
Just as you couldn't live
Outside of it either;
To die of a lack of freedom
Like a lack of air,
Because you aren't imprisoned
But simply
Because the cage exists –
What a subject
For a sentence
Waiting for its predicate!

Unseen

Unseen,
As when you reach out
To count up the eggs in a nest,
Gently touching them
With emotion and fear
Before the hidden mystery
They contain
(Eggs the bird
Refused to hatch
Believing them impure),
Unseen
His hand reaches out in sleep
And topples
A monastery
With every dream,
While the Bird
That moves upon the face of the waters *
Lighter and lighter, less and less ballast,
Rises again from every fall
Till it disappears from sight.

---

* Genesis 1:2 'And the earth was without form, and void; and darkness was upon the face of the deep. And the Spirit of God moved upon the face of the waters.' [Tr.]

Hide-and-Seek *

There go the churches
Gliding across the asphalt
Like sailing ships loaded with horror,
The steeple is the mast
And its sails are swollen
With the constantly
Shifting wind.
So shifting, in fact, that
If you don't watch out
You could at any moment be run
Over by a church
Gone mad,
Scurrying to its hiding-place.

---

* Another allusion to Ceauşescu's plan of urban 'reconstruction' for Bucharest which implied the destruction of the old centre. Many old churches were displaced or demolished. See 'Systematisation', p. 128 [Tr.]

A Chain

A rope twisted like a snake
Knotted on itself,
A chain that
Can gather everything together
And reduce it to a single colour;
A word untranslatable
From one pain to another,
With a different meaning in every place.
What is
This untranslatable word?
A leaf that wants to express
The function of a mammal,
A wall attempting
Photosynthesis,
A glove in the shape of a shoe
For walking hands,
A delicate stem
That trembles to be free
Of its own iron petals:
Solidari-té-tá-ty-tate-nosc… *
The grammar of liquids
That brings out shimmering light on waters
In underground wells,
That knows by heart
The active, passive and reflexive diathesis
(The latter two are almost
The same)
Waters chained, waters bound,
Seeping through quicksands
Without a hope, with no tomorrow, no today,
When all of the leaves
Give me recipes to be saved
Shouting how to cope:

Wither, fall,
Die, die, die…
An ersatz hope.

---

* Allusion to the Polish *Solidarnoşc* Trade Union whose name is translated into different languages: *Solidarité* (French), *Solidaritá* (Italian), *Solidaritate* (Romanian). [Tr.]

Motionless

Motionless, my eyelids closed,
I suffer time to trickle down my flesh
Like an insult well-deserved –
For I can understand, and am
Guilty of understanding, and unnerved.

Impotence invades my senses
Stunning them with
Beads of poisoned mercury –
I cannot act and so, abased
I sink beneath derision and disgrace.

It isn't fear, but futile weariness,
The pain of being late, self-contempt,
Grinding of teeth, with obedient rhymes –
I sift through signs of life and find
A small black pile of words in lines.

Refrain

To those who now begin the journey through kingdoms
In their mothers' wombs
                    (Ah, the future!)
Or maybe they haven't reached there yet
And their mothers are still young girls playing
With chemical elements not yet seeds
                    (Ah, the future!)
I think of them,
Those moments when they want to know
How I managed it:

To those who will be
Unable to imagine,
Unable to see
Through the dirty window panes
Always closed
For decades
                    (Ah, the future!)
Cruel, though honest,
Ignorant of the sale of slaves
And the auction of ideas
                    (Ah, the future!)
I dream of those
Who wonder
How I didn't lose
My life, or my mind,

Those who are still no more
Than a vague desire,
An optimistic wish
                    (Ah, the future!)
They will ask me
In their unknown tongue

How I managed to
Reach them
If I reach them

        (Ah, the future!)

And I'll feel that
I cannot answer
'Through the absurd',
Because the absurd is a concept
That will not translate
From one age to another.

Systematisation *

A yearning for structure
In a landscape of adobe homes,
A yearning for mountains
In hills of waves on end –
Who could ever comprehend
How much has fallen here, and gone?

Wisdom refined
From dung and mud
To fill in cracks between still
Living boughs, delirious,
The same temptation entwines
Soft architraves, sagging sills,
With sculpted columns and rods.

The dream of stone instilled
In the earth as it sleeps,
Scored with waves by rain and plough,
Tomorrow with temples
That bear the fruit of guilt
And, beaten by the sweeping
Wind, will yield and bow.*

---

* This poem laments the adobe architecture typical of peasant construction in Romania which does not resist the pressures of time. The poem is a sarcastic allusion to Ceaușescu's 'Plan of Systematisation' decreed on his visits to North Korea and China in the 1970s. It consisted of a pharaonic project of urban

reconstruction, the Civic Centre, designed to house the President's residence, Parliament, government ministries and the *Nomenklatura*. It is today the second largest single building in the world, surpassed only by the Pentagon. Construction began in 1983 and involved the razing of the historical centre of Bucharest (a fifth of the total area of the capital), the demolition of around 30,000 houses, whose occupants were evacuated on short notice, and the destruction or displacement of nineteen Orthodox churches, some dating back to the 16th or 18th century, unique for their architectural style, six synagogues and Jewish temples, three Protestant churches and two cemeteries (i.e. 'Worms on the Move'). This destruction of the old city centre is a cultural disaster comparable to the total losses suffered by Romania in the two World Wars. [Tr.]

Nameless (1)

Destiny uttered by a belated,
Offended Parca,
Who hates us for
The many gifts
We've been given;
Builder
Of our particular hell
In which days and nights
Constantly cancel each other out,
And never get tired,
And never give up,
So that neither the monastery
Nor its ruin
Is ever finished;
Architect of waves
That rise and fall
Again and again
Only to start all over;
Master Builder
Who surpasses all others
Not through science,
But through your drive to build;
Flying spirit whose wings are tiles,*
Double victim
Of your own work;
Curse
In the wall of letters
That imprisons a people.

---

* Allusion to the Romanian ballad 'Master Manole' which represents the idea
that every act of creation implies a sacrifice. Manole, the artist commissioned
with building the most beautiful monastery, can only do so if he agrees to sac-
rifice the first human being he sees at dawn, which happens to be his own wife.
Once he finishes the building, he commits suicide. See note for 'Ballad'. [Tr.]

Witnesses

Guiltier than those we look at
Are those who watch,
The witness who doesn't stop the crime,
But attentively describes it,
Giving the excuse, 'I cannot do
Two things at once,'
Or, 'The image of the innocent victim
Is more important than his life
On earth.'
There can't be only one or two or three
Who are guilty,
When armies of witnesses watch
And wait for it all to be over,
For the hangman to die of old age in his bed
And the victim be forgotten, a second death.
They wait for the evil to come to an end
As though it were the end of a tunnel...
We hang
From our own question
Like a flag suspended
From a gallows.
Time replies, 'You wait in vain.'
'In the judgement of terrible nightmares
Witnesses also share
In the guilt.'

A Hell

Who could have invented
A hell without demons,
Except for those tormenting themselves?
I feel the need to wonder
And I imagine them
Busy trying to light the fire
In the humid air at the centre of the earth,
Afterwards bent beneath buckets of tar
And pitchforks, and other tools
And then, when everything is ready,
Taking turns to do the job
(Who, today, are the demons and who the sinners?)
As in a medieval mystery play
In which the masquerade doesn't prohibit delirium.
In fact, knowing exactly the time
When you are the demon yourself
Doesn't in any way prove
That the demon doesn't exist.

Also in a Mirror

In a mirror there are also waves,
And their water pours
Into the flow of pleasant days,
Raising their illusion to the shores

Of crisis, of questions, of sobs,
So they'll ebb once more with the swells
Of a castigated sea that throbs
And swirls in an eggshell

From which, when it breaks
Newborn waves remove to a bigger egg
With a mast whose image is sundered
Into bits by mirrors roiling under

A heavy question like a scythe
Cut awkwardly from a cloud:
In the sea's salt waves and tides
The wave of time shudders and writhes.

Full Moon

Come, moon, and wake us from our sleep,
Cast your nets into our waters
And bring us out,
Pour us
Into the insomnia of air!
We may not survive,
Our lungs have turned to gills from so much sleep,
But,
In spite of the risk, wake us
And leave us, alone and free, at sea:
So we can slowly move,
With infinite care,
Forward across the waters,
On the shifting architecture of waves,
A horizon stretched like a rope
Between two hells,
Staring into your lunatic eye, crazed with hope.

Exasperation

The exasperation of running
Towards nothing and no one,
As the blood runs from a wound –
I've learned it from many long histories
Subdued by nothingness,
There where the peaks of the mountains of the world
Batter each other and the overflowing
Rivers of milk and honey
Perish in vain;
The exasperation of thinking
It's absurd and hopeless
To open trenches in eternity,
To build a dome on an island of plants
And a destiny
From ready-made ambitions;
An exasperation that can only put an end to
Humour, misfortune, and the ballad
Through
A voluntary death...*

---

* A metaphor of Romania situated at the crossroads of three empires: Otto-
man, Russian, Austro-Hungarian. Allusion to two foundational ballads of
Romanian literature: 'Master Manole', the artist who offers his own wife as a
sacrifice in order to be able to build a monastery, and 'Miorița', in which a
shepherd is warned by his magical ewe that two other shepherds will kill him
in order to rob his flock. Yet, instead of opposing his destiny, he gives instructions
on how to celebrate his own death, which he conceives as cosmic nuptials. [Tr.]

Beneath the Insults

I don't know who, or how
He raises on waves of hate
Rubbish collected in roads one day
That the current takes away,

So the rubbish is king for a while
Above the dirty foam at the top,
Till he casts it onto the great big pile
Of corpses below, the stinking rot

Of time. Be still and heed
The howling lies of the statue-men.
Kneel beneath the insults and greed,
Whose, why, till when…?

That Old Point

I sometimes think –
That I slip on a ladder
While I dream –
What a shame
That ladder has an end.
Since I can't stop falling,
I could do something clever
To make the fall
Itself disappear,
By dissolving its shape,
Removing it to infinity,
Depriving it of clarity,
From the top, all the way down…
A sudden turn in the flight,
Or a tumble into the depths
Would be the same,
With one condition:
That I manage to put off
That old point
Where I hit the tiles,
With nothing to stop me
From falling faster and faster!

To Strike

I'm not afraid,
But I don't know how
To raise
My voice, or how
To reach out to strike.
And when I ball my fist
Must I also fold in
My angel's wings?
And to spit in a face
Do I have to work up
Saliva and hate
Instead of syllables
And splatter whoever
Is standing next to me?
My wing is bleeding from the split
Between revenge
And the alibi:
I'm not afraid,
But striking out
Seems to be
The greater humiliation
To me.

Gara de Nord

Dirty platform, carefully guarded
After papers exploding in the air,
Two fists handcuffed at a back and
Lots of uniforms, may this rare

Image be the stop-frame emblem
Of hope beneath a colourless sun! To see
Through the spectacles of handcuffs
The future of the verb to be.

Plains

Oh Lord, and me?
The higher the well pole
Is raised towards the sky
The deeper down it goes,
Straining, into the water,
Watching over the plains
Wasted by drought
And, like the ghosts of bustards
That long ago disappeared,
They stand there motionless
With necks outstretched
And listen.

The Statues *

Ramses II's replacement heads
Have naturally multiplied,
Eggs
Incubated by
Time itself, curved
Like a spiral
Devoted to hatching chicks
That make their nest
As soon as they're born
On the neck of a statue
Of an ancient king,
So (in a millennium or two)
All the statues look the same:
Same nose, same eyes, same ears
Popping up obsessively on every pedestal,
Damned statues and nightmares
Tirelessly reproduced through
A natural process.

In the Hagia Sophia
On walls of shimmering faces
The Empress Zoe –
One, two, three –
Changes three heads
On her husbands' supposed necks.
While – what a laughable
And useless event! –
Casimir IV
Surrenders his horse and his body
To Ştefan,
Joan changes her mind on the bonfire
And turns into Mihai.

141

Who and what could bring a stop to
This rolling of heads,
Of foaming manes that crash into the shore,
Architecture in motion,
Grinning masks
That multiply their pain
And each replacement Ramses
Waiting
To obtain
Its pyramid.

---

* Ramses II (1279-1213 BC) used to replace the heads of statues representing other pharaohs with his own. In the 11th century, the Byzantine empress Zoe had her husband painted in the frescos of Hagia Sophia, and his head was substituted with portraits of her subsequent two husbands, whom she also killed. In the Romanian city of Iași, the emblematic statue of Ștefan del Mare (Stephan the Great, 1438-1504), prince of Moldavia, represents in fact the Polish king Casimir IV (1427-1492), which the Romanian authorities purchased in 1880. Similarly, in the centre of Bucharest, the statue of Mihai Viteazul (Michael the Brave, 1558-1601), prince of Wallachia, originally represented Joan of Arc, hence his graceful silhouette. [Tr.]

Model

Oh, the flight of the lonely one
To the One,
In whose image
Rivers flow
And avalanches form –
What terror and bravery,
What loneliness.
When it leaves me
I follow behind
Breathless
Ready for anything,
When it comes back
I hide, afraid,
And try to disappear.
The flight of the lonely one
Away from and towards
The heart of loneliness,
In whose image
The waves of the sea are made!

In Motion

Only a swirling thing,
Only the shape
Of even more mortal fractions
That every seven years,
Wave after wave, disappear –
A yes that grows
From a negation
Always terrified
Yet still alive,
A wave myself,
But a bigger wave,
Always a stranger to myself
And the sea,
Fragment of another fear,
Protective
Stillness in constant motion
On an ever-abandoned
Shore…

One by One

You cannot defend a god,
For that would humiliate him,
And he doesn't defend himself
Because he's above
The notion of defence –
The wave that has swept away
All the temples
One by one
Returns to the sea.
And it tells how beautiful the gods are
And how sweet it was to shatter them
And how easy,
And other waves grow
And dream of having
The power to shatter their God.

Alone

He is the One
Not because, among them all,
He is the true one,
But because
The seed of them all is the same.
In the leaves of the oak,
In the entrails of birds,
In the silhouette of the hare on the moon,*
In the bread and wine,
He is the One.
So lonely
That he gets disgusted
And is born.

---

* In Buddhism the hare is associated with the moon. In Hindu mythology, the hare is the messenger of the gods. According to legend, since the hare did not have an offering for the god Indra, he threw himself into the fire, and in recompense, the gods placed him on the moon. [Tr.]

Measure

The-best and the-worst
Don't exist.
They're nothing more than fantasies,
Dreams without measure
Of good and evil,
Promises
Made to postpone the frightening
Moment
When we might discover
That neither good nor evil
Exists,
And that they're only fantasies,
Dreams without measure
Of some even more insignificant
And more ambiguous
Adjectives.

In Its Scabbard

Those who from cowardice refused to choose
(*The Inferno*, canto three, line 57)*
Will wait for the night in vain.
For it will not fall again.

Time, enraged, has stopped,
Unable to produce more hours
From fear of having to opt
Between twilights and auroras,

And the sand in the upturned hourglass
Of the world no longer falls as before,
Suspended in the air, it doesn't dare
To take responsibility for minutes

That would start the rotation of
The timeless stone that grinds the error
And bring the peace of night on those
Who refused, from cowardice, to choose.

And so, eternally aware of their guilt
For all that they didn't hazard,
They stand beneath the quaking day
Useless, like a sword in its scabbard.

---

* Dante 'ch'i' non averei creduto / Che morte tanta n'avesse disfatta' ('I had
not thought/ Death had undone so many'), *Inferno*, III: ll. 56-57. [Tr.]

Molecules of Calcium

No need to rush.
I have to let the time go by.
Every passing second
Wears away a bit more
Pain.
I have to wait.
Every single wave that breaks
Bites into this rock
I'm chained to.
And every particle of rust
Weakens the chain.
In a thousand years, or two,
The rock will be sand,
The iron links will be dust,
My bones will be molecules of calcium
Dissolved in the water.
This pain will be nothing.

The Art of Dying

Ars moriendi, the wisdom
Of slowly sliding down
The long slopes of evening –
I've learned you patiently
Like a childhood
Prayer,
So I won't be afraid
When the moment of temptation
Arrives,
And will be willing
To pay
The price of the exorbitant aura
The executioner demands,
With so much added pain,
Tortures, abuses, insults and fires
Coming in waves from far away
From countless yesterdays
That you have saved,
Song that shamelessly flows
Towards death,
Ars moriendi…

Earthly Sounds

A different humiliation, unlike that of stones
Trodden, or soaked
During years of dripping,
Turned into clay
And moving constantly
Against its will
Till it changes into sand.
Animal humiliation,
Every cell urges me to shout
But I do not know
Whose cry to use
To terrify,
Humiliation of no one,
Faceless animal
Of the desert,
With a mutilated tongue,
Stuttering
Only earthly sounds.

Fallen from Heaven

Fallen from heaven
As though into the bottom of a well,
Riddled with moisture,
Almost extinguished
And dressed as the moon,
But it wouldn't allow the darkness to
Fall around it, the murky day
Like a viscous, trembling egg white
Round a rotten yolk.
Oh Lord of the stars
Disheartened in space,
Try, if you can, to acknowledge it…

Helter-skelter

What seems to be air to fish,
What they happily swim in and breathe,
For me are the waves that crash into
Altars and make the cemeteries heave,

Only to destroy themselves in turn
With water and muddy sand,
Tumbling statues, cadavers and urns,
Ruins and scaffolds, helter-skelter strands.

Liquid chaos, the depths rise up and inundate,
The sky sinks down, the flood is fate:
I breathe the air where fishes die and
I drown in the waves that they live by.

Inscription

All that you can understand
Is hopeless and lawless and

Everything that has no meaning
Waxes strong from erroneous gleanings.

Head Down

Turn the mirror over,
Pour out what's inside,
Things teem,
Rusted spots that breathe
Stuck to the glass,
Look at the roots of your lashes,
Your face
Scribbled on by successive editions.
Turn it over, upside down,
Shake it well,
So there's nothing left
But the skin of the glass,
Luminous and cold.

Through Non-Being

Branches covered with flowers for antlers,
Floating out of memory, a herd of deer.
And this living eye that regards them now had
Not yet been formed to admire them there.

Silent, unseen, like a thought, they glided by
So smoothly that not one branch was disturbed.
Endlessly they passed, while I, falling
Back to another age, observed.

Drowsy birds were sleeping on the flowered
Boughs of their heads, and softly hummed a tune
Without awaking, even though they sensed a
Troubled cloud. This was my presence in time to come.

It waits for them here, demanding confirmation,
Beholds and will not believe that it's seeing
A herd of deer, with antlers turned into flowering
Boughs, proceed ineluctably through non-being.

A Straight Line

A straight line, nothing more,
A firm line between
The two edges of the page
And the opportunity to speak:
From one edge or the other.
But no, the paper is absorbent,
And instead of a line, a procession
Of worms crawls over
From one edge to the other,
Through the earth ploughed by the pen,
Trembling, indecisive
But tenacious, it
Dissolves both the border and the ink.
Moral:
Do not ask the hangman
The difference between evil and good.

Countdown

When I can't bear any more
I begin to count
(Proof that numbers are better than words
Or,
If not better,
Easier to bear),
So I start to count:
Light bulbs, water taps,
The trees I can see through my window,
The pencils on my desk,
Passers-by, cats on rooftops,
Telephone calls.
But, being more rigorous than words,
Numbers can't be mixed up willy-nilly,
Books with rubbish bins,
Car horns with sparrows,
You have to keep a detailed account,
Whose only merit is,
Apart from the exasperation,
That it doesn't lead to
Poems.

Loneliness

The sea that writhes in the other
Is never as bitter as the one in you,
The wave looks like a little curlicue
Whenever we watch it from afar

And the spasm is the rising tide
That follows the moon going down,
Suffering's a concept others have inside,
Spectacular tremendous storms,

The wound, a cause of envy and fame,
Death, the gateway to Parnassus,
Oh the chorus, singing hosannas
Above the loneliness a voice proclaims…

A Less Charged Atmosphere

Sometimes I try to imagine
A less charged atmosphere,
But I can't,
Because
Neither the eye that sees myths,
Nor the eye that sees cars
Is willing to relent.
And look,
Right now,
An aeroplane
And Nike, the winged goddess
Have collided and crashed
For opposite reasons
Beneath my astonished gaze:
One eye can't explain
The failure of the aeroplane,
The other, the death of the goddess of Victory.
And tired,
They both fall asleep and dream of
A void
Where only clouds and birds
Float by.

The Tomb Unburied

The Pyramid of Cheops
Is the tomb of a ship:*
Its frozen base
Rests
On the fragile sails in which
The winds of non-being
Have trembled for millennia;
It stone apex
Extends the mast
That swayed in the empire of Osiris...
And what if,
Uprooted by a storm of death,
The base of the pyramid
Suddenly began to float
Through its sky of sand,
Like the insignificant tip of an iceberg
Dragging
Its tomb into the air?
Then we'd see
The Pyramid of Cheops
Wobbling unsteadily,
Slipping off slowly and beginning
To sail across the dunes,
Carried along on their crests,
Almost sinking and
Coming up again among the waves
Of earth that hide,
Like those of the sea,
Buried ships...
What a dream
Of an ironic sleep!
But who could stop
The ship,

Once it had unmoored,
Or who could awaken
The dreamer?

---

    * Ships were part of the funeral dowry of Egyptian kings and high dignitaries, such as the one found in 1954, which belonged to the pharaoh Cheops. [Tr.]

More and More

The more I resemble myself, I lack
Myself, the more of a stranger I become –
Intentions killed by the force of facts,
Hope in the mud of guilt undone.

From age to age it has always
Been me, pushing towards the shore,
Wave after wave, I raise one up
Only to shatter one more.

Wave after wave through the sand,
More and more finely ground into scree
The same as myself, my face, my hands,
Less and less like me.

Open Bird

That bird was opened so wide
Above the world
(Just the way a book can be opened,
Even read, but not really understood
Unless you know the language it was written in),
Opened so wide that one wing
Covered the sun
And the other one
Covered the moon –
While men
Tried to make out the will of the sky,
Which they couldn't see any more,
In the bird's naked viscera.

From Chaos

Walls of water, liquid towers, castles
Of boiling foam
Like the transient cities of the sky,
Related they must be,
Towards which they yearn
And almost arrive,
Bursting in slow explosions
Whose ending is long delayed,
Turning the pain
Of their spasms into roars
That thunder on the horizon
Triumphantly resounding
In shining echoes like balloons of foam
And suddenly shattered into shimmering debris,
Splinters of light, deafened suns
Extinguished by fear, and therefore the sign
Of new undulations,
Rhythm of all rhythms
That brings forth from chaos
One dying wave behind another.

Torn Void

The power to choose
Between being involved
And being alone,
The courage to opt
Between the suffering of a scream
And suffering in silence,
The strength to decide
Between fleeing away
And fleeing inside,
You master the universe
In which
The stars burn
Through indecision.
A void torn in two,
Dual eternity
From which
Pieces of aeroplanes and
Slices of angels fall.

Colosseum

The only thing left
Was an enormous fragment
Of the left foot.* On looking,
You could hardly tell
What it was; they had
Placed it in the museum courtyard
Since it didn't fit in any room.
Who could have imagined
The entire statue
Of which only this fragment remained
And a word, Colosseum,
Which everyone now believes
Applies to the neighbouring arena.
The city burned down to be rebuilt
Around this colossus
Hasn't known for ages to be scared
Or to laugh at it;
Only the tourists, enchanted, touch
The gigantic remnant
And read its history in guide books,
Then they stare again:
At the fragment of the left foot...

---

* In Nero's palace in Rome there is a statue that represents a foot, a fragment much larger than a person. This was originally the statue which Nero ordered to represent himself, called 'colosseum' because it was so huge. Today, the Colosseum refers to the arena, and not the original statue. [Tr.]

Clocks on Rails

The clocks stop from time
To time, and then move on,
But those that are driven this way
Don't know that they've stopped
Nor how long they've been still,
Nor how fast they have to go
To recover time lost,
Nor how a void has formed somewhere
And a few seconds may be lounging
In the compartment of an entire day.
While, somewhere else,
Crowds of people rush in waves
And perch on rooftops, stairways, wagon buffers.
Those that are driven this way answer conscientiously,
'I'm forty-two,'
Unaware that some of the numbers are minutes,
And others, millennia,
Nor knowing the names of the stations
Where they stopped
To cross paths with others
Or for no reason at all.

Like Foam

Monarchs on the waves,
Kings floating
On the undulating surface of the crowd,
They stay on top by a miracle,
Against the laws of gravity –
Suspended between two storms –
Like dirty foam
Up there,
The higher they rise
The closer they come to death.

Nameless (2)

We always talk about him
The way you touch the rim
Of an aching tooth with your tongue.
When we forget him, everyone sings,
But his sickening memory clings.
It's always in our prayers, our curses.
We take it in daily doses
Like poison in a spoon
To which we are growing slowly immune.

Charred Remains

Burn the villages, Crişan* cries,
Burn all villages that refuse to arise
And make them fertile fields of flame,
Let disobedience blossom there in time
To kill the final seed of fear,
Raise churches made of fiery frames
And let curses be sung inside!

Burn the villages, Cloşca shouts,
Burn all villages that won't rebel
So all of their patience is quelled
And not one sprig of humiliation sprouts,
Raise castles of flames to the sky
And fill them with audacity
In this century of living centuries!

Horia, alone, is mute, contemplating charred remains:
It cannot all have been in vain, in vain, in vain…

---

* Allusion to the 1784 Romanian serfs' revolt in Transylvania led by Horia, Cloşca and Crişan which became a fight for national liberation from the Austro-Hungarian empire. Horia (Vasile Ursu Nicolea) was a political genius. Knowing that the Romanians would not rebel, he created the necessary conditions for the revolt to take place. He went to Vienna to speak with the emperor, Franz Joseph, who protected the Romanians from the Hungarian nobility, and upon his return he pretended that the emperor had ordered the revolt and subsequent burning of those villages that disobeyed his order. Horia knew that a true leader had to be a mythical figure, aloof and almost invisible, and he acted through Cloşca and Crişan. In the end, they were all betrayed and publicly sentenced to death: while still alive their bodies were broken on the wheel in front of three thousand Romanian serfs who were forced to witness their torture as punishment. [Tr.]

Nameless (3)

Something
(I haven't got the strength
To say someone)
Will someday put an end
To this seemingly endless nightmare.
Then we'll try
To understand
How we fell asleep,
How long we've been sleeping
And how we were able
To dream
Such monstrous forms.
Is our metabolism to blame?
Our enormous
Childhood traumas?
Or maybe this mysterious toxin of
Terror isn't even of this life?
One day we'll wake up
And we'll think
We were dead and we have come back from the dead.

Rhetoric

If I had the sword of fire
In my hand,
Would I take it to the dried-out edge of the world,
With its easily flammable tatters
Of paper and leaves,
Ripe to take the seed
Of the conflagration?
Would I? Would I thrust it into things?
Would I envelop the earth
In its deep red flames,
In its deep black flames,
Beating my wings
To produce enough wind
To quicken the blaze?
If the sword of the end
Were in my hand
And I weren't able
To implant it, would I hold it –
Weeping with outstretched arm –
Far from the dried-out heart of things?
Praying for rains to come,
To put out my torch,
To soak into my robes and
Feathers,
So they begin to rot away
Along with the world
To which I had denied
The purification of fire…

Like Waves

Like waves, monotonous, that break their swell
In this same place, and ebb back to the sea,
The very same crimes, in the very same hell
Are repeated and repeated incessantly,

And when the pace slacks off, slows down,
The hangman gets bored, victim turns abettor, and
The same mechanical, petty game goes on,
Rooted in the womb of the worlds, in every land,

A convulsive game, in fits and starts,
That feeds the turning wheels of power
With blood that waters all of the stars,
And darkens empires in daylight hours,

So it starts all over again, this hell,
With victims from a different coterie
Like waves, monotonous, that break their swell
In this same place, and ebb back to the sea.

Clio*

Falling leaves rushing
Back up to their boughs
While history
Simply rots away,
This shameless, headlong
Flight into death
From which the banners of crime
And lock-step marches descend.

Thus, gentle moments
Packed in herds are beasts
With whose cadavers
The master then builds pyramids,
The master who thought
For those he killed for thinking,
Being more honest
When he kills.

Take from me
The chalice of the sperm of power,
Goddess stuck together with blood,
Decently draped in pencil marks –
Falling leaves rushing
Back up to their boughs
Like an hourglass enclosing
Endless sin.

---

* Clio, muse of history and epic poetry, the daughter of Zeus and Mnemosyne
(goddess of memory). [Tr.]

Glue

What do we lack? What glue
Extracted from the beginnings
Of the sand that moves in waves
Redrawn by any wind,
Or what mortar without which
The wall that rises to nothingness
Will suddenly fall from
The menace of a thought?
What do we lack? Only petals
That aren't a part of the corolla,
And only long threads of wool
That weave no rug,
And only stones rolling through the air
And not turning into a barricade,
Only unmatched despair
Preserved in a sense of humour.
(Like foetuses poisoned
By their mothers' metabolism
And preserved in formaldehyde – proof
And demonstration of a senseless life.)
What do we lack? Glue for bones
Broken on the wheel,*
An untranslatable
Word in the end
That we ourselves were a part of.

---

* Allusion to the leaders of the 1784 revolt of the Romanian serfs in Transylvania, Horia, Closca and Crisan, whose bodies were publicly 'broken on the wheel'. See also 'Charred Remains'. [Tr.]

Thermometer

'The important thing is not lose your head'
They always told me
And I imagined heads
Like little balls of mercury
Nervous, uncontrollable
And always about to lose themselves,
Which I would've liked
To put all together
Into a single shiny globe
Just as I did one time
When the thermometer broke,
Holding its silvery blood
In my hand.
Then I nodded off – I recall –
Trying not to fall asleep,
Obstinately clinching my fist
Around the living seed,
While I heard
Those words of my worried elders:
Let's not lose our heads…

Wooden Language

Why should we insult wood? *
Dead as it may be, it still retains
The structures of life, channels of sap,
Melodious fibers like waves
That years ago ceased their oscillating motion.
Why should we insult wood?
Through it have passed, before they burst out,
The thoughts of leaves, the colours of flowers,
The brilliant and ambiguous chromosomes
That sail through seeds.
Why should we insult wood
By giving its sweet name
To this hecatomb
Of murdered words
Condemned to rot away
In our brains,
This wax museum of syntax
And morphology
In which desiccated truths
Are fixed and stand at attention
And begin to march
(One step forward, two steps back)?

---

* In Romanian 'limba de lemn', in French 'langue du bois', 'language of
wood', means doublespeak or stonewalling, a figurative way of referring to an
ambiguous, dead and meaningless ideological rhetoric. Orwell's equivalent is
doublespeak and Newspeak in *Nineteen Eighty-Four*. This meaning was reinforced
by the French scholar Françoise Thom who analysed Soviet propaganda in *La
Langue du bois* (Wooden Language, 1987). 'One step forward, two back' is an
allusion to V.I. Lenin's book *One Step Forward, Two Steps Back* (1904) which,
together with *What Is to Be Done?* (1902), represent the most important texts on
revolutionary strategy. [Tr.]

Obsession

Would I love you, perhaps, the same
If you were as powerful and frightening
As the others? Would I think of
You as much if you were victorious
And cruel in war?
Would I dream of you,
Anxious, if you ruled over
Others? Just as children
From happy families leave home
When they grow up, without obligations
And can, if they wish, forget about
It all, while the children
Of the poor must always go back
To help their family, send them
Money and packages to keep the little ones
In school, so the happy poets
From larger places
Can forget their roots, go away,
Belong to the world…
Would I be so obsessed with you, perhaps,
If you were happy? If you were able to
Oppress, to conquer, to make people hate?
Oh God of History, give
Them a future beyond these borders! *

---

* Last line belongs to the Romantic poet Mihai Eminescu's 'Scrisoarea I'
('First Letter'), 1881. [Tr.]

Ballad *

I have no other Ana,
I wall myself in, alone,
But who can tell if it's enough,
The wall doesn't fall on its own,
A sleepless, capricious bulldozer cuffs
It down, aimlessly rambling
Through this nightmare scene.
And then I build again
As though I were building a wave,
The second day, one more,
The third day, one more,
The fourth day, one more,
An eternally liquid monastery
Destined to collapse on the shore;
I wall myself in again,
Oh, lime
And brick and beam,
A flawless being,
Armour
Of the ill-starred dream:
I have no other Ana,
In fact, I even have
Less and less
Of the one I am.

---

* This poem alludes to a popular Romanian ballad, 'Master Manole', a metaphor of the idea that nothing can be created without sacrifice. Manole is an artist and the architect of a monastery, which falls down every night. The curse can be dispelled only if he makes a sacrifice of the first person he sees at dawn, who happens to be his own wife. He walls her in, is able to successfully complete most beautiful monastery, and then kills himself. In 'Ballad', the lyrical 'I' assumes both the persona of the artist and of the walled-in wife whose sacrifice enables the construction of the monastery, her body being part of the structure and metaphorically 'armour of the ill-starred dream' of the artist. [Tr.]

CLOCK WITHOUT HOURS

(2016)

White on White

I write in white on white
Though I know nobody
Can read it,
Not even myself,
When I've forgotten what I wrote.
Good is always
Hard to understand –
It's easier to accept a blunder
Up in heaven
Than a noble human sacrifice.

I insist on writing
In white on white
Even if they tell me
To use bright
Letters at least,
When I sketch out olive boughs
Or boring
Good deeds.

However,
Here and now
I've just one colour
That contains
All the rest and I
Write in white on white
In vain.

Times

Before the past
Was the past perfect
And before
The past perfect
Was another past that
Had no start
But was lived by heart.

After the future
The future perfect comes
And after that, the threat
Of another future yet
Which, out of fear,
No one dares to imagine,
As though they believed
It could really be.

Only this moment,
In which you fall away
Eroded by each second,
Exists in this urgent now
With a present to come,
Inside of which hides
The abyss of another present time
Somewhere beyond today.

Nostalgia for Paradise

Evil, like a seed of the world,
Hidden inside a fruit
In the hermetic gardens
Of paradise,
Continues even now
To clone as in a trance
Infinite forests of trees
Of Good and Evil
As though
It couldn't cease
To be amazed
By so many mindless victories,
While it arrogantly offers,
In every piece of fruit,
Another chance for its own defeat,
Which it overcomes
Each and every time.

And So on and So on

I only dream about myself.
Though I'm several other characters
Who terrify each other,
I know that I am always I,
Always willing to dream of this same self.

And even if I wake up
I know it's only a dream
Of waking up
And I can hardly wait to dream that I'm asleep
To be able to dream that I'm dreaming.

How marvellous it is, this game of being myself!
A game without an end!
Because the end
Will also be something I dream and
So on and so on and so on…

Pause in Writing

Great pauses in writing,
Like some bizarre lull
Interrupted from time to time
By intense peals of laughter
Of a crying beast,
Unarticulated sounds
My human ear
Can find no
Meanings for
And it doesn't know if it's deaf
Or if the voice dictating before
Refuses to speak any more
And it feels that the howl in the wild
Is the only expression there is,
Which
I don't know how
To write down.

Heretic

Heretic,
That is, prefers to truth
His much more wavering
Vain and human traits,
He doesn't even pay a greater
Praise to gods
Than the amazing
Similarity
With ourselves.

My soul of the hereafter
Has always been that way:
Much more frightened of eternity
Than of death.

From Mirrors

Do not replace me,
Don't put somebody else
In my place,
Someone you consider to be me
And you permit
In vain
To wear my words.
Have mercy on my words
If you have no mercy on me,
Don't make me disappear
In the face of a stranger
Who shamelessly bears
My name
Without even trying to be who I am
As though
She never had known me.
Don't make believe
That I am I, but changed,
Don't humiliate me by
Erasing me from mirrors
And leaving me only in photographs.

Flow

The ocean swells when night comes on in the hereafter.
It swallows up marshes that seemed to be dry land by day,
Out of them, at times, the bellies of ships emerge
And the slender shadows of masts
That sway in the distance
Above soft plains,
Where at dawn,
One by one,
The fish condemned to death
Will be sown
When the wave recedes again…

One

You are woman and man
(Husband and wife, as Orpheus said)
And yet, you are One,
Supreme and singular cipher:
Woman and man,
A self
United, you dominate
The world of women and men
Who, divided, are not able to
Reconstruct a face.

Only fragments, crumbs, slivers, sand,
Impossible to bind together,
Intertwine forever,
Women and men,
Uncompleted solitudes
That duplicate themselves so often,
Unlike you,
Lord,
Who remained unique and alone.

How sad, this empire you have chosen
Oh King,
Woman and man, in vain!

This Beautiful Time

This beautiful time:
Dark blue sky spread
Out across a net
Of silent lightning,
For the thunder is unwilling
To intrude upon
A dream.

This beautiful time,
Like an oasis formed
In the future eye
Of a storm
Beneath a lid of cloud,
Across which swifts trace lines of poetry.

This is neither
Waking, nor dream,
This beautiful time
In eternity…

At a Pavement Café

If this could be
Something else, not words,
But as full of meaning
As the reaction of the beggar
With her eyebrows plucked as between the wars
Who stared at me defiantly,
As though I had only done
What I should
Or maybe as though
It were my fault that
She had to humiliate herself by begging.
This didn't seem absurd to me
But heartbreaking, and I was happy
When I saw her – she knew that I saw her –
Limping almost gracefully
Towards a table at the café
To order a profiterole, rolling her r's.

I dream of a poem the same as this event:
Or not the event, really,
But the wake of perfume
It leaves behind like a cluster of senses
That will never turn into words.

Disease

Could it be just a contagious disease?
Could time be a virus
That passes from one sick person to another
And leaves deep traces in the flesh it has touched?
Would it be possible, if so, to step back from the epidemic
And keep it from infecting the blood?

Could there be, if so,
Another opportunity
Not to come down
With the eternal disease?

Even though we care for our loved ones
Touched by the affliction
And even though we know that
The immunity is harder to bear than the disease,
And that in the end
It all turns out the same?

Transplanted Church *

It looks like a small and
Delicate animal
Locked inside an
Outsized cage.
The domes,
Used to reaching up towards the sky,
Standing on tiptoe now
Can hardly reach
The band
Of cement and iron
That circles the fourth floor.

It looks like a little animal
That trembles
With fear
When heavy trucks rumble by
Or the deafening gurgle of water
Roars in the cisterns of toilets
In bathrooms looking down from on high
With the wicked eyes of broken
Windows in vertical
Walls,
Wondering what it could be:

It looks like a terrified animal,
With a forgotten pedigree,
Weeping in the void with heart-rending peals,
A little animal
Living still…

---

    * During the 1980s, when Ceaușescu didn't destroy them, he had churches and other singular architectonic monuments of the 16th century transported on rails and relocated among modern buildings where they were much harder to see. The church is like a caged animal exposed to profane and improper noises in a place where it doesn't belong. [Tr.]

In a Wound

We live in a wound
And do not know
Whose body it belongs to,
Nor why.
The only certain thing is the pain
That surrounds us,
Pain
That our presence
Infects
When the wound tries to heal…

Different Languages

His loneliness brought us to life,
His loneliness created the world
So he could bring us into the world
In his proximity,
So he could have someone to talk to.
I knew he invented us and
We exist
To be able to answer him,
But I didn't know
– And He the all-knowing didn't
Foresee –
That we would speak in different languages.

Similarity

In the beginning
The very idea of similarity
Seemed like an insult to me,
Later
Little by little
I became discouraged
And my pride just melted
Like the wax
That waits for a seal.

Now
I'd prefer to look like someone
Or that someone looked like me,
But before
And after
The cipher One
It's night.

Green Icon

Like a green icon
Cut by my window frame
Out of the meadow,
Grass grows on my desk
Between the pencils
It tries to convince
To sprout,
In among the computer keyboard
Proud to be its field.
Its blades form ghostly shadows
On the pages,
Weeds,
Strung together like the letters
In a text that augurs ill,
Like images
Of future wastes
I yearn for.

Silent Film

Unknown seas
Beat their wings
In my ears.
I can feel them rising
With the rising sound against my eardrum
Drawing the curtain of waves
Unheard by all the rest
Between the world and me.

Its sound separates me
From all that surrounds me:
The senseless commotion,
The arguments, the tears, the faces
Desperate and comical,

Like a silent film
When we want to laugh
Without knowing why.

I was afraid

I was afraid to be born,
Even more: I did
All I could
To avoid this terrible misfortune.
I knew I had to scream
To show I was alive,
But I was set on keeping mum.
Then the doctor took
Two bucketsful of water,
One hot and one cold,
And dipped me in
Repeatedly
Like an alternative baptism,
In the name of being and nonbeing,
To convince me,
And I shouted a furious NO
Forgetting that a cry means life.

Nothing Further

Beyond those silken wings
Lowering over the opened eye
Of posterity
There is *nothing further*.
Incomprehensible,
The future-abyss,
From death, the future
Is only a chimera.

The eye that death,
Moving its wings
As though they were eyelids,
Causes to blink
As if it could see,
Is dead.
Only a few moments more –
Tears still flow
From the tinder of eternity
Dreaming of a sunset
Over distant waters
With a port that doesn't exist.

That Year

Small things started to grow that year
And they didn't stop. Nature's laws transcended.
Flourishing growth, perverse, was everywhere.
Birds looked like bulls and their flying ended.

Purselane, nettles, grasshoppers, mites,
Sorrel and burdock, mandrake and sedge
Grew and grew to an amazing height,
Delirious waves beneath the outsized thistles' heads.

Elephants with giant spiders entwined,
Eagles, quite sad, from claws of sparrows hung,
Lions in the desert trembled and whined,
Discordant hymns from puffed-up crickets rang.

Worms in a year to snakes had grown.
A blade of grass became a club;
A speck of dust, a boulder stone.

Always Led

Always led
Towards something I don't understand completely,
Naturally led
As though my hand were taken
By a force of which
I only know it masters me
Immeasurably, and is useless to resist.

I don't understand
Either why
Or where
It takes me.
I go into the mystery,
But the mystery stays intact.
Only I feel it's not the first time
I find my footprints along the way.

Did I leave them there in the past?
Or was it someone else's feet?
Everything is shown to me at last,
Nothing depends on me.

Web

Everything hidden.
The brilliant spider
That weaves its web
Across the entire world
Crouches in wait
And follows its destiny
And its victims –
Itself a victim
Of a bigger web,
Caught in the borderless
Web of the universe
That also hangs…
But from whom?

My Horses

At a signal the herds asleep on the walls *
Descend with a sigh of hooves through the snow,
Above the sky, above the night, above the world
My horses' long green shadows go.

I stroke their manes, their necks, their flanks like springs,
My caresses turn into reins, I put the harness on,
My daring sleigh glides light above the snow,
I recite my verses to spur them along.

The moon says: look, that sleigh flies on its own,
It may be a lunatic, maybe I can help, the poor old
Moon doesn't see my steeds and doesn't know
They passed it long ago.

The wind says: look how that sleigh flies by
Itself, as if it were pushed by an exalted wind,
The wind doesn't see my steeds, poor thing. It doesn't know
They passed it long ago.

All night green shadows of my horses glide,
But at the dawn, back to the walls they flow,
Tame, unchanging, ridiculous there, they fall asleep,
To dream of madcap gallops through banks of snow.

---

* 'Green horses on the walls' and 'look for horseshoes on dead horses' are
Romanian expressions that mean to pursue the impossible, to dream fantastic
dreams. [Tr.]

Curved Tiles

Curved tiles – what fragility!
Almost ready to break
For years, for decades, for centuries,
While whole generations of cranes
Carefully build their nests
In the crevices,
Lay their eggs,
The eggs hatch
And the chicks fly away,
But the roofs remain,
The roofs remain
To wait in troubled sleep
For another generation
Of lightning bolts, of hail,
Of passing birds:
The rooftop of the world
That only desires
To go back and be earth again.

Symposium

Everything concerning
Nouns and verbs.
Trees, much wiser than we,
Rejoiced in
The sun, in the winds, in the rain,
In all that could caress them,
Without asking
Why
The sun goes down,
The rain dissolves into
Blue and green
Puddles on the ground:
Blue and green
From that time and until…

Joyce's Tower

On the high coast shore,
In Joyce's tower,
Joyce
Only spent three nights,
Described, to be sure, in several books
That the visitors
Have no time to read
(And even if they did they wouldn't understand them).
In any case, the guide assures them
That Joyce is a great writer
Without explaining why or whether
This visit will teach them
Anything.
And so
They look at their watches,
Take a few photos
And leave.

On the high coast shore,
On Joyce's tower
The waves break and break and break…

Interior

Flaking silver
On the aged backs of mirrors,
Nymphs and satyrs beneath the falling plaster
Held aloft by overweight angels
With wings too small to
Lift them off the wall.
Look closely here and try to see
Which one to help
And to whom to explain
The obsolete sadness of leopards
Reduced to cats.

Trees

Some are yellow,
Others are red,
And the most courageous
Have kept their green:

The hidden axes of the world
That we see
When one age changes to another
Unfaltering
On an earth draped
In cassocks of leaves
Floating on the waters.

You, Lord, who sows
All beings,
You tell me it's a sin
To feel closer
To the trees
Than to women and men…

In the Shade

In the bitter eternal shade
Of the walnut tree, I chose
A dream that could raise
My soul to the mystery;

Seeking the golden bough, I lay
In verdant darkness, rustling
Overhead like reeds that float away
On the river into nothingness

Through years, decades, centuries
As dead as guttered stars in the sky.
My God, My God, why hast thou forsaken me,*
Alone in parallel worlds close by,

Where I wait to see my figure,
Distant shadow, mistress now,
Advancing through the disaster
Holding the golden bough? †

---

* Palms 22, 1 and Matthew 27, 46.
    † In Virgil's *Aeneid* Aeneas can return from the underworld where he consulted his father, Anchises, thanks to the golden bough given to him by the Sybil. This is also the title of James Frazer's compendium of folklore and religious practices. [Tr.]

Beneath the Snow

They say the snow gives warmth.
Gives warmth?
Are you content beneath the walnut tree
You used to climb?
Do you recognise the town?
As everyone has gone
To harvest strawberries in Spain,
The empty town looks almost like it did
When you were a child,
Except that the dome of the church,
Covered in tin,
Is uglier now.
In spring
The grass will be the same –
You'll see!
I'll come back then to ask you
If it's true that you can hear it grow…

Dissolution

Slow dissolution through the years,
Like a corrosive acid
That I thought at first was a sea
I could swim in with pleasure,
Without
Any fear;

Slow
Dissolution,
No accident, no deviation
From one realm to another, just
Mysterious, infinite chemistry
That you cannot oppose
Because you don't understand it.

But you know
That the only defence
Is to leave the water
And walk on
Farther alone,
As far as you can alone,
But always into death.

The Right to Shade

Don't go to sleep!
Hang on a little longer with
Your eyelids open to the waking air,
Don't let yourself be torn from my side
By the shadowy waters of sleep.
Please don't leave me,
Please don't leave me all alone
Here on this lucid shore
In the unbearable light of insomnia
Where you don't even have
The right to shade,
Because the shade
Is thought to be an assault
On the loneliness of the light.

The Mirror within the Mirror

What kind of mirror is this?
I stand before it
Greedily staring at
Waters moulded by compassion,
Heaps of figures
Writhing in terror,
Rapidly passing by beneath my eyes
And hardly allowing me respite
To search for and not find myself
Among them,
In order to be sure I don't exist,
And I only see
How all of this chaos of
Fleeting parallel worlds
Is poured into me
As though into a mirror.

Facebook

Phrases and gestures galloping by,
Images
Jumbling together manes and hooves
In a grip that could be
A struggle or an embrace.
Only the speed of the delirium counts,
Panting, trying to get back,
But pushed away
By other messages
Hysterical,
The faster they come
The more devoid of meaning…

Message

Indecipherable message.
I can only understand
That it's a message
Or a creed.
I try to decipher it
Without even knowing
If it's meant for me
Or, conversely,
It's a line
From my childhood,
A halo
Wiped out between then
And now
Without being read.

River with One Shore

Death, on whose bank I'm sitting,
Is only a momentary interruption,
Long enough to decide
To step into the ice-cold water
And tread across the slippery rocks
To the other shore.

I'm not afraid of the crossing,
Only of the moment when the bank
I've left behind disappears
Downstream as if death were a river
That can only have
A single shore.

Sketches

Wings made of leaves
Blinking and rustling
Beneath the laws of photosynthesis,
Devouring light, and
Growing from it –

Lord,
Why not acknowledge that
You haven't yet made up your mind
And obsessed by perfection
You keep on looking
In secret
For solutions,
That angels are the unfinished sketches
Of plants
Whose roots you haven't had time to
Put into the ground?

Not Afraid of Loneliness

I'm not afraid
Of loneliness,
I dream of it
And I seldom see
The cautious
Core
Of being that
Urges me to seek it.

What I am afraid of
Is being alone in a crowd,
The awful agglomerations
Of beings unfamiliar with each other
And less and less significant
And as faceless
As grains of sand
In a desert,
As the drops of water
That make a sea.

Minuscule beasts
Amassed in herds
Of strangers,
Indifferent to each other
And each one to himself.

Residues

Everything I don't understand
Remains within me,
Residues deeply deposited
That
The slightest disturbance
Raises up in swirls
Like an upward snow.

Afterwards, drifts of black snow
Yawn with ineffable secrets
Like the monsters
That open their jaws
From the forgotten sands
At the bottom of the sea.

A Game

And if it were all no more than a game
In which he pretends to flow by
And I pretend to stay,
But he remains where he is
While I slip softly away
In compliance with his ancient law
Beneath the timeless sky.

With stars connected by lines that
Trace out meanings fixed, designs
The changing seasons rearrange and
Spin in the ever-fading dance of light,
Announcing the secret verdict in
Their modern tongue, with clever signs.

I am, I'm not, a game, a dream,
I don't understand what was, or what will be.
Hope is a melancholy paradise
Lost in a metastasis,
If I flow, I shall be,
If he flows, I shall disappear,
It all depends on his wish:
Beneath my stars' design, in vain, here
Beneath the double fish.*

---

* Allusion to Pisces. [Tr.]

Why?

Why be afraid? In any case
I'm dying bit by bit along the way.

The path you lead me on in breath
Is a path of many tiny deaths.

Cells light up and then go out
In me, but I still have my doubt.

Will it be the same, in after days, when
I have died and come to life again?

And till that time, how can I know
What and whom to fear below?

Overdose

Exhaustion, like a mortal illness
Born of too much life
As, after August,
Too much sunlight
Causes the leaves to fall.
An overdose of life
Will push me on
In September
To the dream in which
I'll try to dream
October, November, December
Again…

Mândrămărie Blue *

Porch in azure hue
Mândrămărie blue,
Like a pillar, standing high
For all eternity.

Holding up the sky
By the sky's extremity,
Not a cloud in view
Mândrămărie blue.

Crickets and dewy mist,
Fresh milk in a jug,
Swallows' busy nest
Alive with eggs.

The smell of smoke,
Embroidered blouses too,
Road with herds of goats,
Mândrămărie blue.

Beloved and poor,
Village of serfs, you
Will be no more,
Mândrămărie blue.

---

   * *Mândrămărie* is the name of the particular shade of blue in which the serfs of Transylvania had to paint their houses to distinguish them from the white houses of free peasant farmers. The modifier *mândră* has many meanings: 1) it signifies a beautiful young virgin (*mândră-*); 2) it can mean proud, satisfied, content, elated, invested with a feeling of dignity, of conviction in one's own qualities, yet also presumptuous and conceited; 3) beautiful, majestic, splendid, and 4) the beloved. Since the term is virtually impossible to translate satisfactorily we have left it in the original. This poem is a complex word play that recreates the atmosphere of a village of serfs. [Tr.]

Parnassus

What a mixture of gods
That passed their believers
From hand to hand,
Those happy beings
Whose name means
'He who believes!'
While the unhappy gods
Couldn't manage to decide
Where to store away
The souls that hung
As though from boughs
That brought forth fruit
They didn't need…

Question

Wings and claws,
Beaks in the sky:
What can I give,
What demand, and why?

Wings or claws
In clouds, in grass?
A question
Often asked

At random,
No apparent cause,
A kind of temptation:
Wings or claws?

Angels in Their Pockets

So many poets,
With shoes, with ties,
With cigarettes and crowded agendas,
With obsessions, with envy (above all envy)
But also – how odd! –
With angels in their pockets –
Angels that tumble out
When they reach for their handkerchiefs,
Like letters
Scattered in vain.
But placed side to side in a row, obedient,
Carefully revised,
They could turn into words.

Final Exam

Greying haloes, soft and muted now,
Looming clouds of curls on shadowy heads,
Plumes of smoke ascending over darkened brows
Cruelly exposed, and sad.

And sleep interrupted by exhaustion,
Nightmares rotting from too much life burnt
Away – after all, just a common repetition,
For you see, even death can be learnt.

We all advance towards a final exam
That only geniuses fail to pass.

Have mercy, Lord, on these poor men,
Winners of the sacrament you plant
In a place in the sun, green with grass,
A place that I don't understand.

Insectarium

I've always been dismayed
By insects on display,

Pinned and motionless butterflies, hanging
There with beetles and dragonflies.

Nevertheless, what have I done
For more than fifty years beneath the sun

If not run after living words in
Haste, to skewer them on pins,

To stick a needle through poor things
That once were fleeting words with wings,

To pin them mindlessly on a page –
A page like a graveyard, rotting with age.

An Hourglass without Sand

An hourglass without sand,
A form with no end,
Pretending to measure out
Something that doesn't exist,
Sometimes
It flips over,
So that nothingness
Can flow from
One bulb to the other.

Rape

All of them know
My name,
It lights up their eyes with greed,
They come up close,
They look me over,
They hover above my face, my skin,
My own name
Creeps onto my body,
It tastes me,
And then, suddenly bored, it relents,
The light goes out
In eyes that look away
Sated, disdainful,
As after a rape.

Birches

Green flames ruffled in the breeze at
The tip of the candle pointing to the sky,
Amazingly grown from the earth, these
Apple trees bowing around it close by

Confused by their relation
With a vegetal angel, hovering
Most high, wife perhaps, or husband
Of the shade, rival and white lover.

Then it spreads a carpet of leaves as
Autumn turns its green to shining light,
And its love declines into languidness, and
Its sap becomes the blood of the divine.

Like Birds

Like birds, they really look like birds,
These red leaves floating
On motionless wings
Through humid air
This afternoon
With hidden thoughts.
I hear
Time creaking like a pulley
That lifts up seconds and drops them,
Or maybe it's only the cry
Of the leaves…

Between the Seconds

Like a severed blossom
Whose petals are wings,
Remember how you fell
Between the seconds hurrying?

And how the seconds
Rushed like a brook
To help you get to
The heart of the book,

Where burnt-out stars
Are turned into poems
And it isn't too late,
And it isn't too soon

To give up eternity,
Renounce and forgive.
Remember the darkness inside
The book, where it lives?

Sonnet

...And winter will come, and you'll be compost
Here – now the forest's new-born wings.
You'll hardly stir beneath insulting winds,
The only proof that you were.

Whiteness will disguise the work of hate
And death will give you shelter from your pain,
Ancient lightning bolts will flash in vain
And gutter in the gaping mouth of night.

I know the law of life is change, and lessening,
The same for all, and the time
Will come for all to be reborn,

Still, beloved leaves, I mourn for you,
Like relics of the splendid alibi inscribed
On the rotting carcass of a king.

Clock without Hours

They plucked the hours from the clock
The way you'd pluck
Out an animal's eyes
To make it blind.
Instead of 12 numerals
There were now only
12 black holes of the universe
Through which
Could be seen the great
Inferno of machinery,
The cog wheels
Kept on turning
The hands
Groping blindly around the dial
From one hole to another,
Not knowing what they pointed to.

Not knowing that they pointed to
A time without a time –
A time named Never.

OCTOBER, NOVEMBER, DECEMBER

(1972)

Do you remember the beach?

Do you remember the beach
With bitter gravel
We couldn't walk
On without our shoes?
Remember the way
You gazed at the sea
And whispered you were listening to me?
Do you remember
The hysterical gulls,
How they circled above us
In the pealing of bells from invisible
Churches whose patron saints were fish?
The way
You ran towards
The sea and
Shouted that you needed
To be farther away
To contemplate me?
The snowflakes
Melted
And mixed with the gulls
In the water below,
Joyfully, almost desperately
I watched
Your footprints on the sea
And it closed itself like
An eyelid
Closing on an eye, an eye
In which I was waiting.

Wait until October comes

Wait until October comes.
Wait till the nagging fear of
Death that lurks in rutting bodies
Goes away,
The senseless rage of growth
And the blind ripening.
Wait until the bough
Has given up its fruit
And the beast has forgotten
Its grown-up cub.
Stay there in the sky
Until the day
Can brave the shame of
Standing back to back
With night
To see which one is taller,
And the delicate night bends down
So they appear
The same, as sisters.
Do not come close
Until the clumsy blood
Calls out to you:
Descend.
Come only when the tearful
Sun of October rises
From the white-washed egg of the clouds
That brood in warm eternities,
Watch the scales that
Gently bring it down –
And then,
At last, with the face of a man,
Come!

Bitter Body

The smell of a body left by its soul
Beneath the shameless sun.
The smell of a body on which
Flesh is growing,
In which the muttering blood is flowing
And, in a somehow tumultuous storm
Cells with copulating cells are joined…
Do not come close, don't touch me,
My body is poisonous and bitter,
The sun pours over my armpits and
Butterflies are drunk with me, on fire
From the larvae crushed by desires
Too big for them to hold. Run away!
Run away from the arms of this
Profaning cross on which, in joy, I hate
Myself. Do not breathe in my dizzying perfume
When my soul leaves me here in the sun,
To capture and crucify you where I wait.

What Good Is Joy?

Learn not to be happy again,
Learn not to murder again
With smiles and caresses.
A single smile from you
Can kill the birds on the boughs,
The birds that only a certain unhappiness
Could keep alive.
Every happiness wounds someone.
What good is joy in your world?
At night I dream of armies splitting their sides with laughter
While all around we fall like bits of chaff.

By the Gliding of the Moon

I can always tell when you come
Near by the rustle in the birches,
They all begin to shiver,
A bustling instilled
By the unsure
Gliding of the moon,
So tall and slender you are,
And cold.
Trembling, one hand over your
Eyes, you undo copses of trees
Without leaves
And hamlets with no church.
Return,
Come back as soon as you can,
Tell the days to let you go,
The waters to trickle through your hands,
The stars to leave you in shadow,
Close your eyes, the flowers
You look at are fading,
The birds you see are going down,
The waters are receding.
It's not your fault you aren't from here.
Close your eyes,
It's not your fault, my luminous lover,
So tall you are, and slender…

About the Country We Come from

Let's talk
About the country we come from.
I come from summer,
A fragile homeland
That even a single leaf
Can put out
When it falls,
But the sky is full of stars,
So full that sometimes they reach the ground
And if you go close you can hear how they laugh
From the blades of grass that
Tickle them,
And so many flowers are there
That it hurts
Your eyes, dried by the sun,
While fat round suns hang
Heavy in every tree;
Where I come from
Only death is missing,
There's so much joy
That it almost makes you sleepy.

I won't remember any more

I won't remember any more
If there had been a pasture, or a sea
In my hair,
If the birds had floated, or maybe they were fish,
I'll only know that you have come,
And with closed eyes
I'll listen to the rustling of
The wooded God
That fills me with silence to
My ankles, my knees.
Enough for you to move your hand over me
In sleep for the singing leaves to
Grow on me
From the trunk,
Enough for me to raise my eyes
To see you.
Oh peaceful love,
Soft afternoon
Like a grape
That meets its death
In the dreaming heaven of a mouth.

If we killed one another

If we killed one another while
Staring each other in the eyes,
Our eyes, around which our
Lashes form a crown of thorns that
Wreathes definitively
Every stare,
If we killed each other, after staring at each other
With infinite love in our eyes,
And knowing you, I'd say:
Please die,
Please die, my love,
Our death will be delicious,
You, born of the word,
Will be alone with me and learn
The taste of the earth
And feel the beauty of the roots in the sand
That braid through your hands,
With the joy we can never understand
Of not existing for eternity…
And you would say, caressing me:
Please die, my love,
My love with the face of October,
Encircled as in icons
By the nimbus of death,
Please die.
Leave your colours in the flowers and the sky,
Your long hair in the pathways,
And your eyes in the glow of the seas
So you'll know
Where to find them when
You come back…
If we suddenly died together,
Each one killed and killer,

Saviour and saved,
Staring into one another's eyes
Long, long after we could see no more…

I fall asleep, you fall asleep

I fall asleep, you fall asleep,
With closed eyes
Lying side by side
We seem like
Two dead youths who look the same.
Hear how the drowsy sun is rustling
Through the withered grass,
The sky is soft between our fingers.
It leaves a kind of pollen.
The shadows of flocks of birds
Are moving across our faces,
The smell of grapes suffuses us.
Go to sleep.
Don't be afraid,
Our hair, scattered in the grass,
Has begun to take root,
Soon the leaves will wrap us
In golden snow.
We've never looked so much alike.
Your wings have sunk in the dust.
They can't be seen any more.

Brightness of Death

The little bugs are dying in the air,
Smiling
They fall, softly mown, without any pain,
They fall on our shoulders and hair,
The light
Surrounds them all like a shroud
Of brotherly love.
And it beckons the bees to enter the hives,
The bears to hibernate and
The leaves to fall.
Light that shines towards death,
Holy light, light of tears,
Tenderness that overflows the word,
Soft light, good light,
Discovering the splendour in eternity,
Just like the light of the moon,
A clearing in your dreams that tastes of hay,
Of the broken wings of butterflies,
The dried-out pages of books,
A silence that flows
Before birth,
Silence of light,
Brightness of death.

My shadow is afraid

My shadow is afraid of the
Shadows of the trees,
More afraid than I am
Of the trees themselves –
The trees don't dare
To attack me,
But always at my back
I hear a
Savage rustling
Of shadows.
My shadow is afraid
Of the shadows of the birds,
Much more afraid
Than I am of the birds themselves –
The birds fly above me
And don't come near.
But my shadow curls up
And begins to roll, wounded
By the slippery beak of a shadow.
My shadow is defenceless,
It has no roots
Like the shadows of the trees
And it doesn't know how,
Like the shadows of the birds, to fly.
It was brought into the world
To follow me
With the darkness, bleeding,
To end up disguising itself as night
So that I won't know how long
I've been walking around without a shadow,
Singing.

The one in me

The one in me who kneels down to you
Is guilty of that in my eyes.
The one in me who does not kneel to you
Will be banished from my sight.

How calm myself and how reach peace,
Wrapped in delusions like fragile leaves?
Ironic angel, useless your siege
With thoughts and leaves, with whispers and seeds.

In vain my time is running out
In the glass like water from an open spout.
The one in me who does not bow
To you is guilty of that in my sight.

Disgusted and dismayed, I banish and mark
The one in me who does not, as you bid,
Bow down in the pure and singing dark
Of the eye kept shut by the eternal lid.

The one in me who kneels down to you
Is guilty of that in my eyes.
The one in me who does not kneel to you
Will be banished from my sight.

Let me sink in a dream, with no escape,
With no lament, to the bed of the sea
Where I'll dream every year your angelic shape
That will never cease bedazzling me.

Do I have the right?

Do I have the right,
Perhaps, to break
The chain
Begun
At the dawn of the world,
Or maybe even earlier,
With the amoeba-god
Broken in two,
Bathed in light by fish, raised in flight by birds
To reach all the way to my ancestors?
Do I have the right to suddenly say
No
To the long chain of suffering that
Has killed me from father to father
Up till now?
Can I get back to death through them
And tell them
That I've left no one in my place?
Oh yes,
As though I could give thanks
Some other way
For the peace that awaits me
If not by offering them the ultimate peace
If not by telling them: It's over,
Fathers and those who mourn for me,
Nothing ties you
To life –
You're free!
And with that slight gesture
Children use to caress their parents
I shall anoint their faces with the brightness of death
And lead them smiling among the saints.

Swing

Green descends into yellow
Like a gentle swing
Upon which the angels undress and throw
Their wrinkled garments to the ground.
The earth hides in cassocks
Beneath which the thread of night weaves into the world
And grows pure,
Yes, you can only find naked angels laughing
In the woods in October.
With dew on their cheeks,
With blackberry stains on their teeth,
With thorns and leaves all tangled in their feathers
They beckon to us
Without any fear or shame,
Not knowing who we are.
Wherever they tread
They crush some fruit
And point to
The seeds that are destined to be wasted.
We get lost among them –
We are the bride and groom
Of this twilight
World.
The fortunate lovers that never
Were fated to bear fruit.
In their clumsy, somewhat silly way
The angels notice that I have no wings;
Childish, they try to unbutton
The symbols of power on my shoulder-blades
And when they see that they can't,
They angrily bend down
And begin to throw
Fruit and seeds at me…

Alabaster bodies of poplars

Alabaster bodies of poplars emerged from the pond
With soft and somnolent shapes,
Beautiful youths or only women,
Sweet confusion, moistened hair,
They didn't dare to hide their desire,
The water was endless and round,
And the moon poured oil on its
Shining face.
We walked ahead, barefoot and pure,
I felt
My fingers fall asleep in your hand,
There was so much love on the water
That we couldn't sink down,
There was so much peace that the time
Didn't dare to count a beat,
The sky pronounced no clouds,
The water murmured no waves,
Only the naked soles of our feet
As we walked on the moonlight
Made a gentle sound.

Two Suns

We haven't been given
Just one
Single sun
That darkens
Day by day towards the fall,
But, crushed by their weight, we
Carry two suns that
We cannot see simultaneously.
One of them calls us to go in,
The other one beckons us to rise
And go away.
One conjures up a fanatical
Fear of being stopped,
The other goes slowly down,
Invincible, to the end of the day.
One of them watches over growth,
The other encourages decay.
One sheds a light like fire,
The other is more like honey in the sky.
And this is the one
That teaches us the way, and softens
It at night, and digs a sweet nest
In the earth, and carefully cradles death…

With a Soft Despair

Night and the mountains help me,
They grow so tall they disappear,
They rise up in their shells
And stealthily peel away from the earth
Like the bellies of snails.
Everything is silent.
I can feel that they've departed
By the sound of my voice
(It doesn't bounce off
And come back).
My cry for you keeps going
And I hear it
Disappear with a soft despair
When it cannot find you.
Then, for a moment, I hear
How the air opens out
To let it go by,
As if it were not already dead.
The mountains stay there some time longer in the sky
And then they come down, disappointed,
Knowing that once again I wasn't able to find you.

While I Talk

With my teeth clenched between eternities,
Every word is an act of faith
On the broken line
Between the sky and me –
If I talk to you, you have to be.
There in the mountains, where the pine
Trees, like junipers, also grow small,
And the clouds rush over the rocks,
A word rings out in the whirlwind.
I know it is yours,
That tyrannical sound in the depths that
Is lost in the tumult of my blood
Though the pine trees and the clouds hear it.
My love that no one
Has seen except in dreams,
Father of the words within me
And Lord of the unsaid,
Uncertain son,
Born in the prayer
That I raise to you,
I'm tired of so much singing,
So many disordered thoughts,
So many angelical words.
You have no pity,
I cannot see you, I cannot hear you –
While I talk to you,
You are.

I Only Have to Wait

The illness is closer to me
Than I have sometimes been to myself.
Just as the rot is
Closer to the fruit
Than its pit.
Just as the bone waits
Only for the summer to pass
To be rid of the fruit,
I only have to wait
For life to pass away…

Mother

Mother, my first grave,
Burning darkness,
Abandoned with mindless impatience,
While every lump
Of its earth
Resisted that senseless departure.
Will you some day forgive my resurrection,
The hurried resurrection that tore me away from you
So that, light of light,
I could approach another death?
It's getting colder and colder,
Strangeness invades me
While I ascend the pathway back
It disappears.
There's so much distance between us
That churches could be built there
To mediate our prayers.

Light inside Myself

When my inner light begins to shine
Everything around me goes dark,
When the dawn is near
It's night wherever I am,
And I can't look outward
And in at the same time.
I can invent flowers and animals and fruits
Only when I cannot find them.
Nothing I hide in myself has life
Beyond the boundary of myself.
Will it never, ever be broken,
This perfect balance
Sleeping between the world
And my soul?
Is it only because He doesn't exist outside
That I see God so clearly, inside of myself?

Teach Me to Darkly Burn

Let me light myself from your darkness,
Teach me to darkly burn
In that fierce light,
Mould my flame
In the shape of wings
And purge it of any colours.
Or,
Better still,
Give me a seed of darkness
To bury in the earth
And make the seasons spin more quickly
So it will grow,
And bear fruit again.
In that fierce light
There will then be woods and fields,
Copses, orchards, meadows and forests of the night.
A tender darkness
In which we can die when we wish,
A darkness in which
We'll be neither lovely nor good,
But will only be alone,
And without having to look,
Will be able to see when we close our eyes.

You have no shadow

You have no shadow,
When you walk among mirrors
The slightest tremor moves across their waters.
Shadows cannot attach themselves to you
And you
Can't hold on to the shadows in mirrors.
I take your hand
But I'm alone in the mirror,
I only see my nervous smile
Through which passes
At times
An unquiet flutter
And then I know
That, leaning over me,
You've left a kiss.
How will I have to pay
For not being able
To flee?
Oh, have pity,
In other times
They only would've burned me
At the stake.

Crowned with poppies

Crowned with poppies
Almost wilted,
Picked in the morning cool,
When the dew turns to mist
And, as you walk on the grass
You crush the bodies of crickets,
Crowned with poppies,
Running into dying butterflies,
I walk on
Through the dream I call
November,
Towards that uncertain moment
That is neither death
Nor thought.
Enormous rivers flow through the dream
To oceans
Carrying their sleeping fish
In wet and temporary shrouds.

You Haven't Forgotten the Language of Plants

I know, you've only come back to tell me something,
Something the clouds couldn't say,
I know you can't
Stay, you haven't warm clothes
And you haven't forgotten the language of plants,
You've only come to leave on my brow…
A sign that says, 'Good night'.
You get cold and you go away
Without me,
All of the animals of the world
Come near, they see the sign
And they worship me,
The woods bring an offering of leaves,
The lizards, their skin,
But around me there is light.
And then
The animals of the world
Hold me accountable, and make me pay,
The woods draw back and whisper, offended,
You've gone.
You've left no bridge, you've placed
The sign of the night on my face
But you haven't told me
If night will ever come.

Our place

Our place isn't here.
We try in vain to rot away.
The seeds inside of us,
As teeming as pomegranate seeds,
Will not find the soil they need
To take root.
We can't die yet.
We still have to
Suffer this splendour
That lets us walk through it
In our sleep, in deafening dreams.
Our place
Is somewhere far, far away.
Or maybe it's already passed us by
And we just didn't notice it.

You Never See the Butterflies

Haven't you ever noticed how
The butterflies share glances above us?
Or the signs the wind makes
To the grass when we walk by?
If I suddenly turn
The branches are stone-still
And they wait for me to go away.
Have you noticed that the birds are setting?
Have you noticed that the leaves are going out?
Have you noticed the whispers
Growing behind us
Like moss on the north side of trees?
And the silence that meets us everywhere…
They all know something that is hidden from us.
Maybe we've been condemned
Maybe there's a price on our heads.
At night the stars shine nervously
When they hear the rustle of the husks of corn.

If you don't want to come back again

If you don't want to come back again
Beware of the mandrake root –
It steals my voice at night
To cry with
From your footprints;
If you want to forget me
Go hide in the moon –
It will remind you of
How I once walked barefoot
In its light;
If you want to leave me
Go hide in the rain,
Be careful with the snow;
If you want to forget me
Do not go near the sea,
Go round it,
Don't be seen beneath flocks of birds,
Flee
From the long-haired willows
Till you find a place
Where oblivion is waiting,
Hide yourself from everything that lives.
Oh, but if you want to leave me,
If you want to forget me,
Don't try to die,
Above all, don't try to die –
I know how to descend, as if into
A fountain,
Through the flowers…

There was a time when trees had eyes

There was a time when trees had eyes,
I swear –
I'm sure
I could see when I was a tree.
I remember how they looked at me,
The odd flapping wings of birds.
Birds flying by.
But I can't recall
If the birds were aware
Of my eyes.
Today I look in vain for eyes in the trees.
Maybe I just can't see them
Because I'm not a tree any more.
Or maybe they've gone down through the roots
Into the earth.
Or maybe,
Who knows,
I only thought they had eyes
And the trees have always been blind…
But if so, then why
When I walk through the woods
Do I feel like something familiar
Is watching me?
And why, when they crackle and blink
Their thousands of lids,
Do I feel like shouting –
What have you seen?

It's tall and dark in me

It's tall and dark in me,
You can hear the flutter of wings above,
Somewhere, through an unseen window
A ray of light comes in, unutterably staining
The immaculate darkness that surrounds me
And in which I seldom see you.
You inhabit my submissive body
Like a second blossoming
That hasn't yet burst into petals,
Nor reached that moment when they start to fall.
My childlike calamity,
The roaring of vaults is only
The shudder of your wings
In a flight through the seas
Between the window and the altar,
An agonising flight towards vaults of fear
That you might worship me.

I was taught

I was taught the ocean is very big
But not what *very big* means,
I was told the stars
Are overhead
But not what are could mean.
Will we someday understand
The attention with which the sightless
Eyes of the birds observe us?
Will the crickets someday know
Why their songs amaze us
When we don't understand what they say?

Lament in solitude

Lament in solitude,
Bitter snow melted
Into pollen and dust,
Dead on the shoulders of the guard,
Aged from sleeping in the light,
Delicate and bitter snow,
Poor snow,
Indecisive, compassionate cold
That feeds my tender sleeplessness
And soft fears,
Snow that announces a night
Much deeper
Than the day can imagine,
The most tearful day,
Snow mixed with rotting fruits
And with seeds of children.

All the Peace in the Universe

What is there like the void
Between parents and children,
Like the void that opens up in the place
Where flesh has flowered out of flesh,
Like the yawning chasm in the palm of a hand,
Like the navel pulled out by the roots
By the wind
That always blows in the same direction of
The ages?
What is there like the silence
Between parent and child
That look each other
In the face and
Find no words to speak?
Oh, all of the peace in the universe
Is born from the deep silence,
The foaming silence between you and
Your son who has returned from the earth.

Among Leaves That Are Almost Cold

When, among leaves that are almost cold,
I take your hand and touch your lips for silence
So you won't wake up the crippled fledglings in their nests
Abandoned by the flocks that
Migrate to the south,
When the forest begins to shine and
You can see with
A frightening clarity
The sky at the shore of the trees,
When the beasts unveiled
By the flight of the leaves
Cry out and change their colours,
We're tied to one another
And strangers,
As each single eye
Is tied to the other,
As one eye is a stranger
To the other.
The half of the world I see
Shrinks beneath the shield of my eyelid…

Couple

Some of them only see you,
Others only see me,
We overlap so perfectly that
No one can see us both at the same time
And no one dares to live on this knife's edge
Where the two of us can be seen.
You only see the moon,
I only see the sun,
You yearn for the sun,
I yearn for the moon,
Being back to back,
Our bones long ago fused together,
Our blood carries rumours from
One heart to the other.
What are you like?
If I raise my arm and
Reach back as far as I can,
I find your sweet collarbone,
And higher, my fingers touch
Your holy lips,
Then suddenly they come back and crush
My lips, till they bleed.
What are we like?
We have four arms to defend ourselves,
But I can only strike the enemy before me
And you the one before you,
We have four legs to run,
But you can only run in one direction
And I in the other.
Every step is a life-and-death struggle.
Are we the same?
Will we die together or will one of us carry
The cadaver of the other

For a time
Slowly, too slowly, inoculating him with death?
Or maybe he will not die completely
And will carry the sweet burden
Of the other for all eternity,
Withered with so much timelessness
Like a hump on a back,
Like a wart…
Oh, only we know the yearning
To be able to look into each other's eyes
And understand all,
But we are back to back,
We've grown like two branches
And if one breaks away from the other
Sacrificing himself for a single look
He will only see the back he's torn away from,
The bleeding, tormented back
Of the other.

Without you

Without you I'm cold.
I've never understood
How the air feels
After you've left.
The universe gets smaller
Like a broken ball
And leaves its cold tatters on me.
The black dog
With its belly stretched out softly on the snow
Gets up and walks away
Looking into my eyes,
Refusing to tell me its name.
It begins to snow.
It stings my skin
In the spot you've broken off from.
And I'm cold,
When I feel how this prayer
Falls softly with the snow
To no one.

Why not come back to the trees?

Why not come back to the trees,
To the trees stunted by the burning wind,
To be among the flocks of leaves that
Scream like birds,
Among the almost insane leaves,
Mixed in among the hordes of gulls
And ready to begin their pillage;
Why not come back to the trees,
To the beach ransacked by the wind,
To be among the dried-out roe and rotting algae,
Where I can roll as I cry –
Giving myself in tears to
The leaves, to the birds, to the fish,
Beneath the burning sun,
In the salty snow,
Where you see me and leave me.
Oh sea,
My body can bring children into the world,
My soul never.

You Are the Dream

All of them have always loved me,
And those who hated me have loved me the most.
I've always walked among others
Surrounded by love,
Just as I walk through the winter
Always covered in snow.
The law of retaliation is ruthless.
Love seeks love
Just as blood seeks blood,
When it snows
And, lascivious and menacing,
Long, fuzzy ropes of silver
Encircle me,
The snow also asks me to snow.
But I walk through the snow asleep,
You are the dream from which
I do not want to escape,
Distracted, forgetful,
I seldom dream of a look more intense,
The soft snow freezes on me,
It presses against me,
I feel warm and cosy in my dream
And I know that I will die,
And I would be forgiven if
I woke from you,
But I only desire
This slight flutter that
Rises from my closed eyelids.
I go beyond, covered with snow,
Towards the heart of the ultimate labyrinth
Where a fair trial is awaiting me,
A trial that will find me guilty
And, perhaps,

Will punish me for all
The loves that I've missed while I slept.

I had just begun to fear

I had just begun to fear
That somewhere in that rarefied air
The snow would suddenly stop,
I had just begun to know
That you can no longer hide
From these eyes, eager to see,
I had just seen how a fine
Line settled on your head
Trembling in your hair and soft
Over your barely moving eyelashes,
I had just begun to dare to believe that
Those shoulders drawn in the air with
Inextinguishable snow were yours,
And yours the wings betrayed
By the unstoppable snow.
I could have touched you,
But I was afraid I'd shake an
Unexpectedly clear shape
From your invisible being,
I could have learnt you by heart
For that moment
When, the snow falling faster and faster,
You would frighteningly disappear once more…

Which of Us

When you go away
I don't know which of us has gone,
And when I reach out
I don't know whether I'm looking
For myself,
When I say: I love you,
I no longer know if I'm saying it to myself
And I feel ashamed.
Not long ago I knew
What you looked like,
You were
Incredibly tall and slender,
And I knew where you began
And where I ended,
I could easily find
Your lips, your neck,
Your sweet collarbone,
Your youthful shoulder.
Long ago, I remember that
We were two,
I remember that we held hands…
Which of us was defeated?
Who was able to stay?
Is this single body yours
Or mine?
I yearn so much
For whom?
Alone in the silence,
Closing my eyes and my teeth,
If I try hard enough,
I can destroy you
Inside of me
And then I don't know
Where I am…

Sometimes I dream of my body

Sometimes I dream of my body
Trapped in fishnets, in wrinkles,
Dragged through the snow
On the frozen, glittering beach
Of a limpid sea,
I never see the fisherman,
But I know he's your father,
I only see the wrinkled net and
My body, an abundant
Catch.
I tenderly dream that morning of death,
Of a pure, unknown serenity
In which you don't come back,
I don't call out and
Everything sleeps with open eyes,
And the only thing that moves,
Light in light, like an echo,
Is a tenuous curse –
And the net unravels
And I glide once again
Through the timeless immaculate water.

I'm blinkered

I'm blinkered
Like the eye of a horse.
Don't ask me
When I get to you
What trees and flowers
I've found along the way.
I only see the trail
And, from time to time,
The shadows of the clouds
That send me messages
I don't understand.

The fog coming in

This fog coming in,
Is it your eyelid
Closing sleepily on the world?
The world dreams
Beyond itself;
Have I alone
Been left awake
On purpose
To see how the dream
Flows into good, unchanging
Death,
Like a spring that
Sets in the sea,
Just as the stars set
Slowly, slowly embraced by the sun?
To see how limpid death,
At times,
Shivers when it dreams
That I've been left awake
On purpose,
So your eyelid can
Hurt me as it closes
Tenderly on the world?…

Alone and Without Any Thoughts

To be left alone and
Empty without any thoughts
As fir trees and stones
Are alone and naked.
I'll tell my
Ears to sleep
And my eyes to close
Just as
Once
The fir trees and the stones
Renounced their eyes
And their ears.
In the silence and darkness
I hope to be able to glimpse
Through the shining cracks
Of my soul –
The blind and eternal sun
Forced into the snow…

Oh Your Body

Oh I still see your body through the ink,
Ink that stains us even in our dreams
Like bitter animal sweat.
I want to reach you
And my fingers slide,
I can hardly see you,
I can hardly hear you,
Tell me, tell me once more that
The whirlpool I plunge into
Darkens us both the same.
I call to you,
But the ink runs violently out
Between us, as though from a wound.
Do you still know me? Still wait for me?
Will you still let me go back,
Will you still receive me
From the purple mud?
Will you still come back to
These blue fields,
The desert seas,
Speechless and in tears
So I can offer my trembling mouth
And lips, bruised with words,
To your kiss?

Close your eyes

Close your eyes, close your eyes,
We'll only have this once.
I ask you nothing,
The snow is settling,
It's buried the graveyard and the town
It covers the church,
You can only see the tips of the poplars,
Sprouting like grass.
The snow settles and rises
Like a leavened plain
That will soon detain the
Fall of time from above.
Close your eyes,
We'll only have this once
And we can only give it once.
I ask you nothing, wait
For the final flake to settle
And a void to appear in the sky,
Peace, and only then
Remove the nails from your left arm
And slowly turn the hourglass with snow.

Exile

I depart in exile inside myself,
You are my native land
That I can no longer return to,
You are the land where I was born
And where I learned to speak,
In all the world I only know you.
I have swum through your eyes so often
Setting off from the shore, my body always blue.
So many times I've sailed through you
In wait for that babble foreboding the slander
Of the blood that can, at any time, drown me.
You are my part of the earth,
I can only lift myself up from you
Lord, you, full of forests
And sown with lakes,
A territory that I once possessed and
I can never go back to,
Inside myself, my strangeness,
At least let me dream of myself at night
Stepping lightly through your sleep,
Let me inhabit you in the night
As dead geniuses are inhabited by their thoughts.

VARIATIONS ON A GIVEN THEME

(2018)

To R

*   *   *

I knew it was just a suit,
But I had forgotten.
Only when you decided
To take it off
Did I remember, feeling scared,
And I straightway asked myself:
'Why are you afraid?
It's only a suit
Even if, for so many decades
Everyone thought it was you.'
Now, at last, there's no more room for confusion.
There it lay, all wrinkled,
Faded from being worn so long, used up,
Nothing else to do with you,
Away over there, beneath the flowers.
I forgot to look at it,
Feeling that your timeless gaze
Contained it, together with us all,
Useless for you now.
You didn't see yourself
Because, as in Wells's novel,
Only the suit made you visible
And only the snow
Falling onto your shoulders and hair
Betrayed your presence.
But it wasn't snowing inside the church.

*   *   *

I remember wondering once
Whether you and I had two guardian angels,
For since we were always together
Two would have been a waste.
Only one would be enough.
It never crossed my mind
That we might part someday
And then the angel
Would have to choose
Or, perhaps, one of us would have to do without.
Tell me, truly,
Do you regret having left it
Only for me?

*   *   *

Between the spirit and the body,
Between the meaning and the word that hides it
There's much confusion,
As though it were a single indivisible
Miracle,
When the miracle is the division itself,
That moment when the flesh of the word falls
Off the white bones, dried
Of meaning,
And we discover
That the soul has always bound us
More strongly than the blood.

*   *   *

Lately my life seems like a novel by Agatha Christie.

Everything was going along quite normally when, all of a sudden, you mysteriously disappeared.

And then, from time to time, at shorter and shorter intervals, someone else disappeared; and two more had to disappear, then three, for me to begin to get suspicious and to panic.

Not a single week goes by without somebody vanishing and we all pretend not to notice, each one afraid that he'll discover his own disappearance.

You were the first.

Or maybe the novel had already started to unfold, and I only began to read it with you.

*   *   *

Time, at times,
Was suspended between us,
We left it behind
No longer two,
And we understood what the animals said,
Or what the crickets sang,
As though we had safely escaped from
The final judgement.

Or maybe it was just
That two halves,
Separated since the beginning of the world,
Were put together again
Into a single being
In which, just as plants bear fruit,
We were both halves.

Time had no meaning any more and it shattered
Into thousands of leaves.

*   *   *

'I have a pact with the mirror,' you said.
'It has sworn on its life
To reflect you only as I see you.'
And for years the mirror
Was true to its word:
It always showed me bathed
In your luminous tear,
Like a living water
That kept me unchanged
As in fairy tales.
I look in the mirror, terrified,
Expecting the change.
But there it is,
Nothing happens.
What marvellous proof
That you haven't stopped looking at me.

*   *   *

It's as though we met in a bright, transparent
Bubble of soap
That I sometimes manage
To blow,
With the two of us inside,
Happy and beautiful,
Knowing
That everything only lasts for seconds.
In spite of that, it's all so miraculous that
Who knows whether there, inside,
A second
Doesn't last
For thousands of years...

*　*　*

They sway, they sway, those heavenly
Sounds, not yet moulded to melody,
Words that whisper rhythmically
The void of forgetting to be.

A quavering serenity
Cut precisely into slices
Of the customs of times
Gone by, on which the living glide,

Words that were long ago orphaned
Quoting the spectres of their parents –
I listen now, an adult, intense
Among children who were forebears then.*

---

* An allusion to Mihai Eminescu's famous poem 'The Epigones' (1870), in which he compares himself and his contemporaries to the poets of old, and considers the latter to be happy and young because they have faith and hope, while, on contrary, he and the poets of his generation are sceptics and believe in nothing. Thus, the ancestors are children and modern poets, exempt from hope and faith, are prematurely old.

*　*　*

If there were microphones in houses, like before, the listeners would surely think I'm crazy when they recorded me talking with you about all kinds of things, asking your advice, telling you the news of the day, saying *I love you*, like that, in the present tense, and *good night* before I switch off the light.*

Or if any of them were new to the job and didn't know you'd gone... the fact that you didn't answer me would raise their suspicions and they'd think that the pauses in the conversation were signals they couldn't decipher.

---

* During the Communist regime (1947-89), the Political Police, Securitate, used to place microphones in people's houses so as to control people. Blandiana herself was under surveillance. [Tr.]

*   *   *

Without you
The world seems suddenly much bigger,
Much bigger and as pointless
As an unfurnished room
With some of its walls
Torn down, without which
I can't describe how
It used to be.
I only know that there's nothing
On the horizon,
Not really knowing what the horizon is.
As far away from a useless past
As a future in vain,
The present isn't a gift for me,
But only a captivity.

*　　*　　*

When I say, 'To those in their graves',* a silence comes inside as though I couldn't go on without knowing who they are.

And only when I'm sure that none of them is you, do things go back to normal, to the customary, to repetition, and the song continues to flow around me harmlessly, as cool as the water we listened to together without being sure it existed.

---

* Allusion to a chant sung during the Orthodox Easter service: 'Christ is risen / from the dead / trampling down death by death / and bestowing life/ and upon those in their graves.' [Tr.]

*   *   *

What if we decided to dream about
Each other, both at the same time,
As though we had a meeting in the dream?
Why haven't I thought of this before, this
Place in the middle, between two extremes?

We only have to fix the time
And the place of the meeting,
However, whenever, wherever it is,
We shall be the lovers who are sleeping

On the razor-thin edge of
The knife between parallel
Worlds, that writes and kills
While thrust into love to the hilt.

*　*　*

I'm afraid of the darkness
At the heart of the flame
Because I don't know
Whether it gives birth to the light
Or the light gives birth to it:
Incestuous relationship
Between good and evil
That crops, through splendour,
Carnivorous flowers of shadow.
I'm afraid.

*　*　*

I don't understand.
What's more: I know it can't be figured out.
But nevertheless, your presence
Is here, beyond all doubting.
Though it may be only a heretical error,
It's the same as it was in the biblical scriptures.

I will not doubt. I don't want to put
This hand I write with in the wound
When I feel you come into the room
Like a fearless, flawless knight.

And as though it weren't so strange already,
I will not ask you how you came,
I don't know whether it's a miracle or sin,
It's enough to feel your presence, coming in.

*   *   *

'Where is the Gentleman?' the old women asked me at the market when they saw me without you, the old women you bought dill weed and parsley from, and when they had it, celery.

'The old women in the market asked about you: Where is the Gentleman?' I told you when I got home; and it made you laugh and you felt so proud that I forgot to add that they said you shouldn't have left me alone.

* * *

What splendour suffering gives us!
The haloes of the saints
Mean precisely that.
Light seeps out
Of the suitcase with your papers
Like the blood
Of a dismembered saint.

*   *   *

Now I pray to you,
You're the station on the way
Of which I only know it exists,
You're the rest stop where my words
Turn into a different alphabet.
I pray to you,
Not knowing what to ask for
Except for you yourself,
And you transcribe my words without understanding
Them, and slowly send them on.

*   *   *

What is love, if not the impossibility of separating two beings who have decided to be together?

Pure and simple, at a certain moment I felt that everything was decided until death. But that last word is only a convention, like any other border that can be moved up or down or abolished by law.

And what is love if not a universal law that abolishes borders?

*　*　*

It isn't true that 'Every Angel terrifies',*
I've never been afraid of you
Although I knew who you were
And could hardly wait to fall asleep
To be able to approach you,
So your aura could greedily encircle me
And overpower me
Like an electric shock…
And even now,
When it's all so much harder to decipher,
And my senses refuse to signal your presence
I'm not afraid, and I go to sleep,
A luminous cloud of mist in motion
A gust of air
That doesn't stir the leaves.

---

* 'Jeder Engel ist schrecklich', the first line of 'The Second Elegy' of Rilke's *Duino Elegies*.

*   *   *

I suppose you can also see it now,
Just as you saw it in your mother's womb,
The wall of darkness
Impossible to describe.
It's just a supposition, for I have no prenatal memories
And I find it embarrassing to imagine
Something that I haven't yet experienced.
However, what I'm trying to believe
Is not what you're looking at
But the fact that you can see.
Whatever there is before and after the more
And more uncertain borderline
Of the senses,
And beyond
The beginning and the end
Of my poor alphabet...

*   *   *

I've thought about what I'd like to tell you
If you came back
And I've reached the conclusion
That I wouldn't present you with words
But images.
I'd like for you to see how
The crowns of the trees slice their forms
Into the sky through my window
Before the darkness falls;

Or that bush with blood-red flowers
Set among the thorns,
Close to where you're smiling in a photograph;

Or the landscape of meadows with
Tall haystacks
That we looked at together from the train
On the way back from Sighet...

Messages that can't be put into words,
Secret messages of the ineffable,
Proof of the supreme truth
According to which
It's enough for lovers to gaze.

*   *   *

The leaves are falling…
Do you have seasons too?
They're prettier when they fall
Than on the tree.
They glow
When death catches fire within them
Like a candle flame inside
A cathedral dome.

The leaves are falling,
Lighting up the universe
With their all-consuming aura
Of parallel worlds.
Do you have seasons too
In which
Beauty is a pogrom?

*   *   *

Is it easy to be dead?
Is it harder to be alive?
How will I bear the time ahead when
The time where you are has gone by?

Tell me how I should act instead
To be the way you are:
It's easy to be dead.
Being alive is hard.

The universe is black
Beneath an empty sky,
I don't know how to turn my back
On life, I don't know how to survive.

It's harder to be alive…

*   *   *

Voices muffled by leaves.
It's wonderful not to know what they say.
I only know they exist
And that maybe they talk to each other,
While my incomprehensible voice
Makes those who hear it happy,
Even if they don't understand;
While you, yourself, speak perhaps
Without us being aware,
Without expecting anyone to hear you
In this realm of parallel sounds
And of joys that need not have each other.

*   *   *

Everything begins with death.
But we just don't know what it is.
And we prefer to confuse
The mystery with nothingness.
Only when a loved one
Who may be a part of you
Crosses that dividing line,
Is everything lit up
In the space of a lightning flash,
And you see how long the road is
That begins exactly there.
So long that
You can't see where it leads
But it doesn't really matter.
What matters is it all begins again.

*   *   *

'I'd like for us to die together,' you said; and I answered laughing, 'Do you think it's right for me to live seven years less than you?' But you were serious. 'How else could we find each other in eternity?' And your logic was so convincing I agreed, half in jest, that it would be a good idea to die at the same time.

Now I also wonder, as serious as you were then, how we'll be able to find each other, where and how I could look for you in the beyond. The only possibility would be for you to wait for me at the border, but I can't tell you when and I'm not sure they'd let you stay there till then.

It seems more likely that we'll search out each other for eternity in the chaos, just as we did on earth, till we're lucky enough to come together again.

*   *   *

Just as unwritten thoughts
Leave only an ambiguous trace
In the memory
Like a trail of footsteps
In the sand that took them in,
Our passage through letters
Is only recorded
In the substance
Of those who soon will have been.
What a fragile posterity!
Sometimes I imagine myself
As the pages of a manuscript,
Like leaves
That can rot and be used
As compost.

*   *   *

I often wonder if what you knew here is useful there, where you are now, or whether you have to learn everything over again, like coming into the world and learning to walk and talk.

Maybe in order to get into the other world you have to be born again (*to come into the world* means precisely *to be born*) and (just as we can't remember what we were before we were born) you won't remember anything about this world that was ours.

And still is mine.

*   *   *

Why won't the moon let me sleep?
What is the connection between its face
Impassive, rolling round the sky
Like a coin over the asphalt ground
And this, my miner's obstinacy,
Descended from the gods, displaced
Now from the other realm beyond?

What makes up that strange light's power
That keeps me awake on the shore
While the river of sleep flows
Happily to where you are
And I feel myself crumble and cower

Beneath the bewildering weight of weariness
From the waking thought on a page,
Broken like the gospels into verses,
While you, my Very Shining Lord of the Deep,
Slumbering for all eternity's ages,
Search for me in sleep.

*　*　*

I've always
Dreamt of being by myself
Because I've always
Had so many people
Around me.
Only you were I.
Only you renounced the plural,
The multiple of two,
Only you knew how to construct a loneliness
Big enough for both of us.

*　*　*

In the phone, your photographs from spring. I remember the day I took them so as not to forget how the trees had burst so vividly into flower. An almost defiant white took hold of us in the air, while the colours of the daffodils, hyacinths, golden trumpets, tulips and that red bush we brought back from Târgoviște rose up from the ground.

'It's not enough for us to be happy,' I said, 'we have to know that we're happy. We are happy, say it, we are happy.' And you repeated, 'We are happy,' and you smiled with an infinite sadness, as though joy were a misfortune that beauty only made worse.

I look at your photos from that day in the telephone, moving my fingers over your face to enlarge them by caressing you, larger and larger, till only an eye remains on the screen, where the pupil reveals, like a sick animal, a foreboding.

*　　*　　*

Nothing stands still,
Death is not what it seems,
A paralysis, a halt.
Disappearance here is appearance
Somewhere else, with a different purpose.
Always in motion,
Existence and nonexistence
Come together
As they go
And they push you along as on a sloping plane
Towards another universe
Where you do not stop
Before the royal gates
But you slide, you slide farther and farther
And more and more surprised.

*   *   *

Your smile above the TV
Like a map of time
On which the screen is the present
And you, the past and future.
They all occur simultaneously,
Ages go by at the same time,
The insubstantial gives meaning to eternity
Framing your smile
Above the TV.

*　　*　　*

Just as somewhere in Africa – I don't know where – the natives pray to the fire they've built, I invent you and then I talk to you.

I ask you for advice I pay no heed to, I read you my manuscripts and don't change anything I've written.

What's important is to feel you close to me, after I forget that I've invented you.

*   *   *

If you feel forced, as I fear,
To cross over Lethe,
The river of oblivion,
You'll look back at me
Without seeing me
And you'll hear me
Without understanding what I say
Nor what the syllables braided
Together at random mean,
It will be as though
You weren't dead
But I had died for you.
A reversal of planes
That would leave me only
My pain, like a dowry,
Like a jungle with birds and animals
Growing from those memories
That you have forgotten.

*　　*　　*

Do you remember when you buried the seeds of the sequoia in the ground, those enormous, masochistic trees that live for more than a thousand years and have to be tortured to grow? People help them by drilling holes in their trunks and filling them with burning embers, and they feel good among the flames that cannot defeat them.

Do you remember how you put those large, mysterious seeds in the ground, like containers to transport suffering that you smuggled through customs?

'Are you going to wait a thousand years for them to grow,' I asked you.

And you replied,

'Why not?'

*　*　*

Sleep is as mysterious as a road
That brings different lives together:
The one before birth,
The one after death
And the one from now.

The sleep of life
Consists of small fragments of death,
The sleep of death
Is a kind of resurrection at times,
And the sleep before being
Is the very substance that separates
The ages.

All three lives only
Communicate through sleep.

Please let me sleep, then,
My Very Shining Lord,
And not be alive any more,
So I can begin to descend,
Go back together to the original void,
While I dream that you remain
Eternally awake
To begin all over again.

*   *   *

There is a law – the Babinet-Mayer law – which says that the rivers
in the northern hemisphere erode their right banks and deposit
sediments on the left, or maybe it's the other way round, what
matters though, is that this way, they move very, very slowly, from
left to right, or the other way round, without us noticing or suspecting
a thing.

How could I rebel because I can't find you again, when the rivers
also move?

*   *   *

I'm not certain you can hear the sound of
Crackling leaves like a murmur in the mind,
Unless it reverberates through the ground
In the moistened footsteps you've left behind.

I'm not certain you're still concerned about
The birds, the branches, butterflies and bees
Or you still understand the eternal
Return to the cradling home in the sea.

Maybe there they make you put out the strands
Of light that bind us to one another
So that I can't hold you back with these hands
In the web of our enthralling love.

Maybe there love's not the same, and lacks
The force that moves the stars and the sun:*
Only a statue of salt looking back
Among us mortal, dying ones...

---

* Allusion to the last line of Dante's *Divine Comedy*, 'L'amor che move il sole
e l'altre stelle' ('the love that moves the sun and the other stars'), *Paradise*, canto
XXXIII, l.145. [Tr.]

*　*　*

Why instead of darkness
Is there light,
A milky light
Where outlines are blurred,
And even though I know it exists
And that you are there among them,
How can I know it's not in vain?

Tell me if I can someday understand,
If they let me
Understand
That, even when we cannot see each other,
We belong to the same time,
The same nimbus,
That we form a part of the same whole

Where darkness is a light
Too bright to be seen
When past and future merge
In the seed of the same core.

*　*　*

We're alone
As we always have been here,
Happy to be alone,
Fearful of guests,
Obsessed with writing and the passing of time.
You're still a part of this
And you make me use
The plural by mistake.
But maybe it isn't a mistake
When the essence of loneliness is the same.

*   *   *

I don't know how to pray
Because I don't know how to beg
Or to praise.
In fact, I'm not even sure
There's any point to
The words between us.
Better to bend my head back
With my neck so tense it hurts.
With my eyes looking into yours,
Pantocrator.

*   *   *

Every gesture of mine
Traces a tenuous strip
Of light, that I can feel
Without seeing.
It's like a continuous embrace
From someone like me,
But it envelops my shape
And keeps me warm.
What an ingenious way you've found
To avoid abandoning me…

*   *   *

On holidays I feel you closer.
Do you have holidays, too?
Or do you only come so
I won't be alone
When everyone else is happy…
Your smile moves through the room
Like a patch of sunlight
And makes the cat uneasy
With the feeling that something strange is going on.

*   *   *

When I was small, just like other kids, I had an imaginary friend. No one could see him but me.

He was a teddy bear dressed in waistcoat, tie and chequered trousers, out of which stuck his head and four chubby paws made of brown felt.

The fact that he was invisible for everyone else and that, when I talked to him around others, they only heard my words, didn't make me think he wasn't real, just the opposite. He was mine, and mine alone. I couldn't go to bed in the evening without saying 'Good night' to him; I couldn't eat anything he didn't like.

That was a wonderful game. Why should it be macabre now? The fact that the neighbours hear only my voice through the wall is one more proof for me that we're a single being.

*   *   *

They ring and ring, again and again,
Like water in a cup made of tin,
The same words ringing in the skull
The same monotonous refrain
Till the feverish meaning dulls
And freezes in the brain.

And the hours and days, the years and more,
Devoted to confession before
Lose their seed and wither away
In the rhythmic, obsessive decadence
Of failure, without a ray
Of motive or sense.

*   *   *

All of the questions,
I've asked them too late,
When those to whom
They were addressed
Couldn't answer any more.
I don't know why I was waiting.
Maybe it wasn't a postponement
But just that the questions
Are only born
When there's no one there to answer.

*　*　*

I've read a lot of books
About the miracles that can happen
Above and beyond the stubborn facts of being,
Proof that so many people
In the same situation as mine
Have tried not to separate completely.
Say something!
Learn from the fervour
Of those who dream of escaping,
At least a single word,
So I can build a bridge
Between this firm ground of mine
And your syllables of water:
Waters flowing
Towards a shore that lies
Beyond the sea...
Where
They disappear...

*　*　*

Where are you, really? Of course, I don't mean the smile above the
TV, nor by any means the bouquets of flowers that left stains on
the gravestone. What I want to know is where you come from when
I call you and where you go back to.

Should I try to find the place in books, as the Egyptians or the
Greeks imagined it? But it would be hard for me to think of you as
one among a crowd in Thebes or Eleusis, and I prefer to dream of
you alone.

Don't worry if you can't tell me; it was only intellectual curiosity.

*   *   *

Where do the hours go?
They have this suspicious way of passing unnoticed,
Drawing no attention
And simply disappearing.
But what does it mean *to disappear*?
How can something that is
Just cease to be
As though it had never been?
Where do the hours suddenly go
And, above all, where do they come from
Like paper boats
That softly float
On a sea like a work of art
With waves that were drawn by heart.

*   *   *

As usual, I spent New Year's Eve alone with you. And, as usual, we talked a lot, especially me.

I watched the fireworks through the window and wondered why people feel obliged to be so happy on this night.

Then I fell asleep and I felt as though I was flowing into you as into a sea.

'Good night, sweet Prince. Tomorrow morning an era will begin when no one knows but I that you still exist.'

*   *   *

I cannot see your light against the light.
I signal to the glow again and again
But the rays all scatter like bright and
Glittering coins, cash to bribe the sun.

My eyes are blinded in this blinding light,
And though I feel your presence all around me
I cannot decipher your silhouette and
Feel lost in the flames that surround me.

I'd like to go back, but I don't know how
From this blinding eternal shell,
A home for you, a pathway for me, where

I dream of a shade that keeps me living
Still, and waiting in this redeeming now
That I offer you in fear.

*   *   *

Snow! It's snowing!
And it means I'll see you
Because your invisible shape
Will take on form beneath the flakes.
So please, stand still
And let it fall
On your shoulders, your head, your hair.
I only want to see you there,
I really do.
I know I can't caress you;
My hand is warm
And would melt your snowy form.
Yes, snow is falling from eternal ice
And the coldness bathes us
In its warm, consoling disaster.

*　　*　　*

The life in your diaries is almost unbearable.
Although I'm familiar with the things they describe,
I'm amazed at the way you write them.
It's just like your mother's despairing soul,
Everything seen in the darkest light.

As though the queen ant chose only weeds,
You never took notice of infinite chance,
The suffering comes back again and again,
Reproducing itself in a self-fulfilling dance.

It spreads like oil over water,
Like a game between love and distraction,
Thoughts grind suffering as though it were wheat
Beneath the ceaseless millwheel's action.

From childhood to the grave your words tormented
And crushed each other in this cell,
Measuring without understanding the whole sweet
Sound of the sea in a shell.

*   *   *

Perhaps the word love
Is too broad, too confusing,
Too imprecise for what there is between us.
It may have been right a long time ago
When we were two,
Two beings
That came together in the storm
Not knowing
What would happen but
Only feeling it would happen to us together.

But now, decades later,
When there are no more distinctions
Nor dividing lines,
No matter how fine,
And the word *soul* has no plural,
To say *I love you* creates a division,
Underlines a difference
That no longer exists in thought,
A step back
From the only creature able
To embody us both,
As though we were determined to know
Which of us has died.

*   *   *

You fell, distracted,
Into the abyss that suddenly opened in the sky,
You began to rise
While I watched you, fascinated,
Not understanding what was going on,
The way you kept getting smaller and smaller
In the light from the depths of that high cliff
From which, I'm sure,
You cannot see me, either.

*　*　*

You can only die in the present,
You don't die in the past,
You don't die in the future,
You go out of time by chance,
As though through an invisible wall
That you didn't see
And after that
You don't
Know how
To get back.
Or maybe you're just not interested any more.
I watch you disappear
By mistake,
More and more indifferent.
Without fear
With longer and longer strides
That echo like a cathedral
In this new present…

*   *   *

Our parents and grandparents died,
Our friends have died,
And we watched.
It was something that always
Happened to others
And we couldn't imagine
Even as a game
Being in their place.
In fact, we couldn't do so
Even when it happened to us,
Neither of us
Believed it
And we waited together for it to come.
Or maybe it was only I
Who was waiting.

*   *   *

Do you understand what it means?
Now do you understand?
Since you continue
TO BE
What is this passage between eternities?
What is the difference
When it's clear at least
That it's not a simple question
Of *to be* or not *to be*?